~

THE AMERICAN DREAM
IN BLACK AND WHITE

THE
AMERICAN
DREAM IN
BLACK
&
WHITE

THE CLARENCE THOMAS HEARINGS

JANE FLAX

CORNELL UNIVERSITY PRESS

ITHACA AND LONDON

First published 1998 by Cornell University Press

Printed in the United States of America

Cornell University Press strives to use environmentally responsible suppliers and materials to the fullest extent possible in the publishing of its books. Such materials include vegetable-based, low-VOC inks and acid-free papers that are also recycled, totally chlorine free, or partly composed of nonwood fibers.

Library of Congress Cataloging-in-Publication Data

Flax, Jane.
The American dream in black and white : the Clarence Thomas
hearings / Jane Flax.
p.   cm.
Includes bibliographical references and index.
ISBN 0-8014-3575-7 (hardcover : alk. paper)
1. Thomas, Clarence, 1948– .   2. United States, Supreme Court—
Officials and employees—Selection and appointment.   3. Judges—
Selection and appointment—United States.   I. Title.
KF8745.T48F58   1998
347.73'2634—dc21   98-34449
                                                                      CIP

Cloth printing   10   9   8   7   6   5   4   3   2   1

To my students at Howard University:

Your courage and grace in a hate-filled world continue to inspire me.

I am grateful for our conversations.

CONTENTS

ACKNOWLEDGMENTS

In the three years of work on this book, a network of friends has sustained me. I owe a great debt to Kirsten Dahl, whose friendship is one of the major gifts in my life. I also am deeply grateful to Joan Retallack for nurturing me with wonderful conversations and lovely dinners. Fred Risser sustains me with care and counsel. Mervat Hatem has been an oasis of sanity, and I am thankful to Rick Seltzer for his humor and computer advice. I owe special thanks to Janet Adelman for her timely wisdom and consistent encouragement to keep my own voice. Barrie Thorne and Peter Lyman have inspired creativity in the art of shaping a life, and Jerry Hartman has amused me. JoAnn Reiss and Victor Wolfenstein have paid attention in special ways. I am grateful to my son, Gabe Flax Frankel, for the pleasure of watching him become a real mensch.

Intellectual work requires conversation, and I appreciate colleagues' providing challenging ones: Anthony Elliott at the University of Melbourne, Temma Kaplan at SUNY Stonybrook, Linda Nicholson and Liz Burnworth at SUNY Albany, Wolfgang Natter at University of Kentucky, the Institute for Clinical Social Work in Chicago, the Association for the Psychoanalysis of Culture and Society, the Institute for Research on Women at Rutgers University, the writing group (Shelley Rockwell, Pat Crowe, Deborah Blessing, JoAnn Reiss, and Joyce Lowenstein) and the floating panel (Jim Glass, Victor Wolfenstein, and Fred Alford). Maureen MacGrogan kept this work going, and my current editor, Alison Shonkwiler, has been just the right combination of critical reader and midwife.

J. F.

THE AMERICAN DREAM
IN BLACK AND WHITE

American Dilemmas and
the American Dream

But if we are fair, this is not, as I said at the beginning, the nomina-
tion of a justice of the peace to some small county in some small
State. This involves the very integrity and fabric of our country.
—Orrin Hatch (Committee 4:214)

Senator Hatch's assertion that the "very integrity and fabric of our
country" was at stake is more insightful than perhaps he realized. The
Thomas hearings were a moment when we were directly and power-
fully confronted with some of the most important contradictions in
contemporary American politics. We have a dream. Our dream—our
very integrity—depends on the ideas of freedom and universal equality. As Americans, we understand ourselves as individuals with
rights. We are all equal. As American political subjects, we each have
a place.

Of course, the story is more complex. The fabric of our country has
been woven out of contradictory threads. Since the country's founding, this dream has depended on inequalities.[1] Race and gender are
two of the most pervasive and tenacious of these inequalities. In our
common-sense understanding, race and gender produce stable identities. Skin color determines race, and anatomy determines gender.
Each is an organic, physical characteristic. We have, however, begun
to understand that race and gender are not biological givens. They are
not natural qualities, but social ones.[2]

Our country affirms its commitment to a race- and gender-blind society. Yet, at the same time, the effects of race and gender on all subjects in contemporary America remain inescapable.[3] Race and gender
define; they continue to determine how Americans are variously privileged or subordinated. Despite the thousands of volumes, speeches,
legislative acts, efforts of organizations, executive orders, judicial

remedies, town meetings, task forces, and commission reports, inequalities persist. Why has the American political system been unable to eliminate these inequalities?

I see two important reasons. First, America's political institutions have depended for their legitimacy on the notion of a particular ideal subject. This American subject is an abstract individual. How can this representation always be accurate? It cannot. Despite the surface abstraction, the normative American citizen has always been a white man and, though others have won rights, he remains so.

The exclusion of female subjects from citizenship and the legitimation of slavery were written into the contract that created the United States—the U.S. Constitution.[4] Although the country's founding document distributed power to and protected the freedom of some, it also ratified preexisting positions of inequality, powerlessness, and civic death.[5] Although neither race nor gender is any longer grounds for denying formal political rights, each remains the basis of multiple forms of privilege and subordination. If we are truly to "face up to the American dream,"[6] we must take full account of this interdependence of domination and freedom, privilege and subordination.

Second, our existing definitions of race and gender are inadequate to grasp their simultaneous, interdependent, and mutually forming effects. To treat race and gender as independent social relations is a persistent error. Some writers claim they can accurately discuss one while, for clarity or simplicity, temporarily placing the other in the background. This inevitably produces a deeply flawed account. In the United States today, there is no ungendered but raced person or gendered but unraced one. Neither race nor gender is extrinsic to the other. No "women" or "men" exist who are unmarked by race.[7] Race and gender are not identical, nor can they be reduced to one thing. They are mutually formed, unstable, conflicting, constantly mutating, interdependent, and inseparable processes. Throughout this book, I use "race/gender" as a linked word. Race and gender may have had separate lines of development in the past, but now each blurs and bleeds into the other. Only interwoven can these ideas begin to capture the complexities of their mutations.[8]

Linking the terms allows for a more sophisticated understanding of current social relations; however, it still cannot fully capture their complexities. Each subject lives out, resists, and remakes race/gender in his or her unique ways. Abstraction is necessary for analysis, but it makes race/gender appear more solid than it really is. What looks fixed is only a temporary congealing of historical practices. Dominant groups may define, but subordinate groups transgress and redefine.[9]

The population of the contemporary United States includes an ever-increasing variety of race/gender positions, each with its own origins and relationships to others.[10] In this book, I explore four of these socially determined and determining positions: white/male, black/male, white/female, black/female. These positions are pivotal to understanding American politics. As a result of slavery's role in the founding of the United States, thereby shaping the meanings of these four positions, they remain essential, and they reveal threads of America's contemporary fabric.

THE CLARENCE THOMAS HEARINGS: A PUBLIC DRAMA

My imagination was transfixed by the public hearings held by the Senate Committee on the Judiciary concerning the nomination of Clarence Thomas to the Supreme Court. On June 27, 1991, Thurgood Marshall announced his intention to resign as associate justice of the Supreme Court. Then-President George Bush nominated Clarence Thomas to replace Marshall on July 1. The committee's hearings on Thomas's nomination extended from September 10 to September 20. The committee voted 7–7 to send the nomination forward to the full Senate. Its vote was scheduled for Tuesday, October 8. In preparing for the first hearing, committee staff discovered rumors about allegations of sexual harassment against Thomas. Initially these allegations were not linked to Anita Hill. Until after the first hearing, staffers had no concrete evidence to support the allegations. Most of the committee did not know about these rumors until, gradually, more specific information emerged. On September 23, after complex negotiations, Hill faxed a statement detailing her allegations to committee staff. Her statement was somehow leaked. On Saturday, October 5, Nina Totenberg read parts of the statement on National Public Radio. The public release of Hill's charges caused enormous political controversy. The protests forced Joseph Biden, chair of the committee, to arrange a second round of hearings. Their purpose was to provide additional information for the Senate, whose vote was postponed until October 15. The second hearings were held from October 11 to October 13. Two days later, the Senate approved Thomas's nomination by a vote of 52–48. Transcripts of the hearings are available in four volumes published by the committee.

What could we learn about contemporary American politics, I wondered, if the transcripts of these hearings were the only available evidence? Of course, this is a thought experiment; as one cannot really abstract in this way. The exercise yields surprising results, however. The material is extraordinarily rich and unusually wide ranging. These hearings are political dramas, not unlike those of classical Athens or the historical plays of Shakespeare. One can learn a great deal about this country by paying attention to this drama's characters, story lines, and dialogue, both overt and covert. Dialogue during the hearings reveals a great deal about race/gender and about guilt, (conscious and unconscious) memory, hate, power, and the politics of both national and subjective identity. These hearings are evidence of the living presence of slavery. Its reverberations, and especially its effects on the contemporary generation of race/gender subjects, can be tracked in our political unconscious. These transcripts illuminate how we use hate in binding communities and in consolidating national and individual identities.

I am not interested in matters of "fact," guilt, or innocence. This book is not about who told the "truth." Far more interesting to me are the process of representing oneself and others and the politics of constructing and interpretating meaning. Both this process and these politics are revealed throughout the testimonies of Thomas, Hill, and others. We can see them play out in the senators' statements and dialogue, even among themselves. The interplay between the senators and the principal and secondary witnesses also is revealing. Especially in the second, nationally televised hearings, the participants are quite aware that their audience extends far beyond the hearing room. This was more than a hearing on Thomas. The redemptive power of the law was at stake; objectivity and individualism were in question. Who defines the meanings of American history, and whose narratives will be accepted as truth? What story can contemporary Americans tell about ourselves? Such story telling is a way of establishing our national identity.

The hearings have had a continuing, powerful effect on public imagination. Much has been written about them[11]; but their meaning and political resonance have not been fully understood. Their impact is incomprehensible without detailed and careful attention to the effects of race/gender. Race/gender, both evident and disguised, is everywhere. It is both in the script and between the lines. It affects the participants and the public. The hearings took place within a context—where both race/gender and the putatively abstract individual were central to the functioning of the American political system. To comprehend their emotional charge, we must also consider this background.

The Constitutional Limits of American Politics

Part of the fascination of the Thomas hearings is watching what happens when issues that have historically been excluded or denied erupt into the center. The very appearance of the hearing room is a condensed version of contemporary American politics: fourteen white/males seated behind heavy wooden furniture, looking out at an array of persons difficult to order. Bits of American history—lynching, intra- and interracial relations, and stereotypes of black male sexuality—intrude. The tensions within race/gender loyalties are evident. We notice the obvious inability of normal legislative procedure to contain extraordinary material and persons (despite the senators' best efforts). The senators try to conceal but nonetheless enact anxieties about their own abilities to comprehend and represent changing political subjects. These anxieties burst out in dialogue, exceeding the senators' conscious control.

The hearings exemplify a major problem facing our polity. Existing democratic processes are inadequate to address contemporary political demands. A central function of contemporary states—the production of appropriate subjects of politics—either has broken down or is severely compromised. Subjects of politics means something broader than "political subjects." I refer to the constitution and representation of citizens and the aspects of subjectivity accepted as nodes of, or loci for, political discourse and action. I also mean the issues deemed publicly actionable and the distribution of public power. Our normal institutional democratic processes are not suited to comprehend, integrate, or contain what they were meant to control, exclude, or deny. As recent controversies about the relevance of our president's personal entanglements illustrate, we lack useful ways to talk about sexuality. Discussion of race/gender is often muddled. We resist talking about the ambiguous qualities of "facts," "knowledge," and "expertise." Can our political institutions deliver on their promise of freedom and equality for all? There may not be room for the excluded, and their pressures for freedom and equality disrupt our country's stability and generate a profound sense of disquiet. The result is a wish to contain or expel all disturbing "difference." This is the anxiety that fuels backlash movements, ranging from attacks on affirmative action, immigration, gay rights, and abortion to the forming of militias. The committee's treatment of Anita Hill provides a dismaying example of how dominant groups try to keep the peace.

CONTEMPORARY IDENTITY CRISES

The United States is primarily a nation of immigrants and slaves. From the beginning, internal conflict and inequality mark its history and culture. Its contracting founders and heirs participated in the displacement and death of the territory's native inhabitants and the importation of slaves.[12] The nation was founded through rebellion—a transparent act of will. The United States came into being literally through war, contract, and convention—the constitutional convention. It is a human, temporal, and secular creation.

Consequently, the prevailing narrative of our founding *is* the founding. The foundation is potentially very shaky and unstable. Under such conditions, our contract (the Constitution) and the legitimacy of the contracting parties are extraordinarily important. Only certain kinds of individuals can make a valid contract. Only certain actors can represent and enact the will of all; they must act on behalf of universal principles, not their own interests, and be "abstract" individuals.

Operating behind this mask, however, the original and still definitive subjects of the American political system are white/males. Challenges to their power to represent and contract for all, therefore, become serious public concerns. Threats to the normative status of white masculinity undermine the political subject that has given American politics its grounding and legitimation. The "white male" problem is literally a matter of state.

Thomas and the members of the Senate Committee on the Judiciary both avoid and manipulate raced/gendered subjectivity. The inadequacies of liberal notions of subjectivity, difference, and justice are evident as the senators and Clarence Thomas interrogate (and do not interrogate), each other and themselves. The senators contest the "true" meanings of race/gender. They also grapple with permissible forms of difference and confront the extent to which (acceptable) differences must be incorporated—meaning either preserved or erased—into existing institutions.

White masculinity was a central, unspoken problem in the hearings. The country's stability was at stake, and the conditions for its legitimacy were irreconcilable. Our institutions produce, require, and depend on a hierarchy of raced/gendered subjects. To maintain its integrity, however, this foundation must be hidden. The senators were uneasy because they were temporarily forced to recognize their own race/gender position. The country cannot publicly acknowledge that this position is the basis of their power and so the senators had to undo this unusual, public race/gender marking and reassume a mask of abstract individualism. Moreover, it needed to appear that anyone can don the mask.

TOXIC TWINS: ABSTRACT INDIVIDUALISM AND IDENTITY POLITICS

Thomas's nomination confronted African-American leaders with one of the most controversial issues in contemporary politics. Is identity in some sense "natural"? Is it a matter of skin color, sexual prac-

tices, or anatomy? Does any set of sensitivities or political commitments necessarily follow from a particular set of experiences? Such
questions challenge feminist and gay/lesbian activists as well. Is the
representation of black, female, or gay interests necessarily advanced
when a visibly similar person attains a powerful position?

The transcripts show that fully contextualized accounts of subjectivity are not possible within the rules for coherent liberal discourses.
The material necessary to provide such an account is split off, denied,
or projected onto others. The treatment of Anita Hill during the hearings revealed theoretical and practical weaknesses in our ways of
thinking about race/gender and sexuality. Complex thinking about
sexuality remains outside of the sphere of legitimate knowledge.
Dominant discourse denies the interweaving of sexuality, race/gen-
der, and power. Advocates of black politics often fail to acknowledge
issues of gender and sexuality. (Feminists and subordinate sexual
groups are sometimes equally reluctant to face issues of race.) These
failures contributed to the substance and outcome of the committee
hearings. There is little space in which the complexities of black/fe-
male subjectivities can be spoken or recognized. The committee
members and many witnesses were unable to find a narrative that
rendered Hill's presence comprehensible; they simply could not locate a tolerable place for her.

THEORETICAL TOOL BOX

I have found many theoretical tools useful in thinking about contemporary American politics and the hearings: contemporary discourses of sexuality, feminist and critical race theorizing, postmodern
and contemporary political philosophy (especially about justice and
multiplicity), and psychoanalysis. Unlike liberal subjects who are abstract, rational, and uniform, psychoanalytic ones are multiple, passionate, and propelled by unconscious impulses. Nevertheless, both
approaches share a common flaw: both lack an adequate account of
the productive and constituting effects of race/gender. The investiga-
tory tools of psychoanalysis, such as defense interpretation, are help-
ful. They uncover the hidden operations of race/gender within mod-

ern Western liberal subjects' constitution. Although the tools of psychoanalysis are useful in this endeavor, psychoanalytic accounts of subjectivity are inadequate. Psychoanalytic subjects do not exist in the abstract. Lacking a recognition of the centrality of race/gender, psychoanalytic accounts of the constitution of subjectivity remain flawed and inadequate.[13]

I value the psychoanalyst's sensitivity to the importance of fantasies, especially about sexuality and subjectivity. The transcripts of the hearings reveal an extraordinary and extended public process of free association. This drama was an ongoing, formative interplay of sexuality and race/gender within the American political unconscious.[14] Acts of displacement and denial are as interesting as overt speech. One remarkable feature of the participants' testimony and the senators' dialogue is how they deny personal experience or even knowledge of sexuality. Another is the prevalence and manipulation of familial (especially paternal) imagery.

Narrative is a major theme in this book. Through narratives, humans literally organize their own subjectivity. Without these organizing stories, experience is simply a "raw feel." We have no way of comprehending or remembering it. By telling ourselves stories and listening to those of others, experience gains meaning and order. These stories may change; experience does not compel some particular version of "what happened." Even to ourselves, we may tell different stories about the same event. Often stories function unconsciously; we are not aware of their ongoing effects. Sometimes only confrontation with alternative accounts makes us aware of our own. Our stories affect what we experience and how we interpret it. Retelling our life story, shifting our narrative of it, may change our subjectivity; and, conversely, as our subjectivity shifts, we rework our old stories. Creating new stories makes different experiences possible.

Narratives shape and make intelligible social practices. These practices accumulate and form particular social worlds, which makes the stories we tell about them very important. Any subject has available a limited array of preexisting narratives. Like language games, these narratives precede us. Developing them shapes us as subjects. Rarely do subjects have equal power to determine the dominant stories of their society. The power to narrate a practice is the power to shape it.

Changing the story about a practice alters its meaning. For example, consider the issue of forced sex in marriage. Is forced sex rape or a marital right? We can tell very different stories about the same act. Which story will dominate depends on race/gender arrangements, but the dominant story also strengthens certain power relations. As alternate stories become available, more subjects are likely to resist. In gaining power to create stories, we also generate new "facts." While sexualized coercion has long existed, "sexual harassment" only emerged from a particular narrative that gained force through feminist struggle.[15]

Feminist political theorists such as Wendy Brown, Carole Pateman, Linda Zerilli, and Christine Di Stefano examine the dominant narrative of modern Western politics—liberalism. They point out that the coherence of liberal politics depends on the exclusion of many subjects. Our contemporary idea of masculinity is partially constructed through its "opposite": an irrational and sexualized femininity. Male bonding arises from and depends on a mutually reinforced understanding of masculinity and femininity. Motivating and animating this bonding is a deep unease about desire and sexuality. Anxiety about the homoeroticism of male bonding is disruptive. This anxiety therefore is displaced onto a more accessible and equally powerful fear of women and the potential vulnerability that comes with desiring them. Male eroticism is thereby denied and projected onto females. Female subjects then become the evokers, bearers, and enactors of sexuality as well as related irrational passions, such as fantasy, fury, hate, jealousy, and revenge.

These processes of denigration, erasure, and projection help define, by contrast, the rational, ungendered, disembodied individual. These are the characteristics of the modern liberal citizen, which are especially important in forming his identities as citizen, political representative, law giver, and judge. The modal citizen, therefore, is implicitly a man. Narratives of citizenship are interwoven with independence, autonomy, and agency. An ability to support oneself, as early property requirements for voting show, is intrinsic to the meaning of citizenship. Citizens are supposed to have control over the basic requirements for survival. Also important, however, is that citizens are potential soldiers; they must have the capacity to submit to and exercise the disciplines of war. To be successful there, their bodies must be rendered docile and asexual.

Carole Pateman's work is particularly important to my own analysis. She argues that the original contract, which both gave birth to and legitimated the liberal state, was the result of bargaining among male subjects. These men were in fact not individuals but heads of households. Part of the bargain was that paternal power would remain the principle of family relations. The contract ratified and legitimated women as property. It authorized the subjection of women's bodies to permanent relations of coercion. Paradoxically, another part of the bargain was the disembodiment of politics. It consigned the "natural differences" among male citizens either to the economic sphere or to the family. By being defined as rational bearers of abstract rights, citizens' bodies supposedly reside elsewhere.[16]

Recent work by Judith Butler, among others, on the social construction of sexuality is equally important to my thinking.[17] Like Foucault, Butler stresses that anatomy, desire, gender, and subjectivity initially are independent. Anatomical features do not invariably determine identity or desire. If we do not believe that identity is rooted in certain, stable, organic characteristics, we must think about other aspects of subjectivity in equally complex ways.

Masculinity, as currently practiced in the contemporary United States, requires and reinforces race/gender dominance. The control and exclusion of female subjects are essential to maintaining and reproducing masculinities and cross-race gender alliances. The plausibility of abstract individualism also depends on excluding females as normative subjects. Female subjects are still struggling to construct femininities in ways that go beyond simple resistance to fraternally controlled meanings.[18]

Power relations, as Foucault delineates, are not fixed or immortal.[19] They are circuits of knowledge norms and practices that require constant maintenance. Male bonding is one example of such "capillary" modes of power. They are constantly renewed and reformed, and the circuits that sustain them are often covert. As in the Thomas hearings, however, capillaries occasionally bleed in public view, exposing aspects of their operation. Such events offer rare opportunities to track the flow of circuits of power.

A fundamental question motivating my investigation is one raised by both feminist and critical race theorists: Are our liberal discourses and practices redeemable, or are they inextricably pervaded by irreparably racist/sexist relations? If the latter is the case, dominant ideas will inhibit rather than empower transitions to more just practices.

This question is both important and problematic. As stated, it assumes that power is exercised only in formal political institutions. This idea—which Foucault calls the "juridical" notion of power—is no longer adequate to comprehend modern Western politics. Analysis informed by this question tends not to consider a crucial feature of modern Western politics: the shifts in the nature of power itself. The putative issue in the second round of the Themes hearings—sexual harassment—is a particularly illuminating example of the intersections of and conflicts between juridical and new forms of politics—biopower.

My analysis is deeply indebted to the work of contemporary critical race theorists, such as Henry Louis Gates, Diana Fuss, Derrick Bell, Patricia Williams, and Cornel West.[20] From a critical race perspective, the ideas of Pateman, Butler, and Foucault provide necessary but not sufficient narrative lines for understanding the peculiar constitution of American democracy. The notion of contract must be reworked to allow for some of Foucault's notions of power and conflict. A contract is a continuous process. American history is full of recurrent conflict, often violent, over who is eligible to participate. Bargaining over the sexual contract becomes even more complicated when male subjects have to (re)negotiate across race hierarchies.[21] As Bell points out, the survival of slavery in the American contract was an intrinsic part of its negotiations. Slavery is a particular way of creating and training docile bodies. The citizen had a right to both the labor and the children produced by slaves and often, of course, some of these children were his own.

As writers such as Paula Giddings, Kimberle Crenshaw, and Patricia Williams argue, sexuality and pleasure were also implicitly negotiated.[22] Who could be the object and who the subject of desire? Who had the power to name and construct identities of both themselves and others? Though shaped by them, black/females have no positive place within dominant discourses. They are defined as less than fully female. Instead, they are seen as overly sexualized objects. Raping a white woman is seen as violating white men's property. Being accused of raping black/females never led to the lynching of black males or to the sanctioning of white ones. Until recently, the language of rape did not even apply to black/females, who were believed to be oversexed. As oversexed beings, they literally could not be raped.

By using the language of lynching, Thomas evoked more anxieties than he probably realized. He asked the senators to reconceive their race/gender loyalties. Sexual harassment is highly problematic, for it represents the revolt by female subjects against men's collective power to define the limits of acceptable behavior. In finding one of "their own" guilty, the men would have simultaneously exposed and undermined the workings of patriarchal power; however, for white/males, to incorporate black/males into equal status as citizens would imply their equality as men. Full citizenship for males requires equal access to all females, including white ones. Allowing devalued males into patriarchal power does not necessarily disrupt current arrangements. These newly admitted males become honorary white/males. They can be enlisted as allies in the struggle to maintain existing power relations. Participation in, if not control over, the "exchange of women" is an important perquisite of masculinity and basis for alliance among male subjects.

Can a black/male enjoy the benefits of the sexual contract? As the Thomas hearings confronted this question, a resolution emerged. Thomas became an honorary white/male. This allowed the senators to rescue a central element of the American dream. They preserved the abstract individual by excluding disturbingly different subjects from relations of power. These elements included a particular black/woman but, by extension, all people of color, white/women, homosexuals, and ethnic groups. The Thomas hearings suggest that without profound transformations in contemporary American politics, for many its dream looms as a nightmare.

CHAPTER ONE

American Dream or Nightmare? Horatio Alger and Race(d) Men

> Finally, I just wish to mention my own delight at Judge Thomas's success. That success says a great deal about our country and about Judge Thomas, the man. Having grown up in the era of Jim Crow and gone barefoot in the unpaved streets of his community, he will soon be able to put his feet under the bench in the highest court in this land as he contemplates the finer points of the law. I understand this. I was born into a family where we didn't have indoor facilities either during the early years of my life. And I understand what it is like in this great country. And I have to tell you, Judge Thomas, I am so doggone proud of you I can hardly stand it. I think it is terrific thing that you are nominated to this position, and I personally will support you with every fiber of my being. As you yourself said when nominated, only in America could such a thing happen. It is wonderful to be a citizen in this country, and it is wonderful to see you sitting there before us this day. And it just reconfirms what all of us already know. This is the greatest country in the world.
>
> —Senator Hatch (Committee 1:43)

The first Thomas hearings show what a central, almost magical, role the idea of the abstract individual plays in America. Thomas is constructed according to the cherished narrative of Horatio Alger. Through his own effort, Thomas has transformed himself from a barefoot black boy in segregated Pin Point, Georgia, into the ultimate abstract individual—a judge. In turn, Thomas's triumph over adversity warrants the believability of American greatness.

There is an irreconcilable tension within American political life. The legitimacy of its institutions requires that all citizens be equal; yet, its inhabitants occupy distinct race/gender positions that deeply affect their life chances in ways that are not voluntary or random. Senator Hatch's opening statement illuminates one way that the American political system finesses this tension. The statement illustrates how persistent aspects of American political life—poverty, inequality, and race/gender domination—are not considered part of its character. At the same time, these aspects are actually celebrated in that they are transmuted into evidence of the country's greatness.

THE FUNCTIONS OF ABSTRACT INDIVIDUALISM

A story so well established and cherished as the mythic Horatio Alger narrative can produce this magic. This narrative teaches that our individual circumstances are irrelevant to our ultimate fate, that there are no intrinsic barriers to individual success, and that failure is not a consequence of systemic structure but of individual character. Conversely, it also teaches that success is independent of privilege, that one succeeds through individual effort and that there are no favored starting positions that provide competitive advantages to those who occupy them. The narrative teaches that we all act independently, that we can transcend circumstances to reach the "American dream," and that it is not even a dream but an achievable reality defining America's unique greatness. The story also teaches, however, that as individual subjects rise to success, they must conform to certain expectations. As citizens, they must strip off their particular histories and social positions and become abstract individuals, unmarked by any race/gender position. Such positions are irrelevant, even a barrier, to their standing under law.

Within this narrative, abstract individualism functions as a manic defense. Manic defenses enable subjects to ward off and deny anxiety-producing or identity-disorganizing aspects of subjectivity. In this case, abstract individualism permits some subjects to disavow their dependence on race/gender arrangements. This disavowal is important because otherwise the correlation between the distribution of social resources and power and race/gender positions would be evident. The existence of structural inequalities undermines the claim that privilege is a simple reflection of the virtue and efforts of its possessor.

By studying when and why the theme of abstract individualism appears, we can track how it anchors fundamental American political ideas. At the same time, we can see how race/gender makes abstract individualism intelligible. This abstract individual cannot exist without its disavowed other. Concrete race/gender subjectivity and abstract individualism form an essential dichotomy. At various points in the Thomas hearings, this dichotomy was constructed, evoked, or recurred; at other points, it simply erupted. The abstract unmistakably depends on the particular.

Subjects in dominant and subordinate positions both have deep investments in race/gender. While Thomas and his supporters were eager to construct him as an abstract individual, they did not hesitate to make use of his race/gender position. From the first, they alternately played and erased the "race card." It is important to recall that the first hearing occurred in September 1991 before the public airing of Anita Hill's charges. Thomas invoked race/gender long before his famous charges of a "high-tech lynching," in a speech in the second hearing that was held the following month. Confined within current race/gender arrangements, it is understandable that Thomas used these tactics. Despite his claims to abstract individualism, Thomas could not escape how he was viewed by his white/male questioners. Although he could not completely elude his race/gender position, he could skillfully exploit it. Thomas manipulated his race/gender to ward off questions about his self-representation and criticism of contradictions in it. He attempted to control the questioning by evoking residual white/male guilt. This benefited his supporters as well. Thomas's use of his race/gender position enabled the dominant narrative to survive intact. Naming him the only person marked by race/gender enabled the relationship between other positions and power to remain hidden. The implication was that race/gender may disadvantage certain subjects, but it does not empower others.

In the first hearing, Thomas and the senators replicated the originary liberal contract. This contract is a bond among particular male subjects. These subjects agree, for specific transactions and within certain conditions, to define themselves and engage with each other as abstract, rational, "stripped-down" (equal) individual political actors. During these transactions, the subjects' race/gender positions are unmarked. Together, Thomas and the Judiciary Committee negotiated a narrative that positioned Thomas both as an honorary white man and as an abstract heroic individual. Since the coherence of individualism depends on implicitly equating white and unraced and masculine with ungendered, this bargain posed no contradictions.

If Thomas were no longer racially marked, he was an honorary individual—a white/male. His racial particularity was split off. This was possible due to invisible but necessary background operations that produce the liberal individual. Masculinity and individuality are linked via race in that only white/males are fully masculine. Simultaneously, this link enables the race/gender of the individual to disappear. White is unraced, and masculine is ungendered. Therefore, as a white/male, the abstract individual is unmarked by race/gender. Whiteness, masculinity, and individuality are all associated with the mind, not the body, and with the capacity to exercise reason, objectivity, and fairness. Because his race/gender is unmarked, the citizen is apparently stripped of all empirical, determining qualities.

Having universal access to the position of individual/citizen is part of the American dream. Thomas and the senators constructed his life story as proof that this dream can come true. It "reconfirms what all of us already know," said Senator Hatch (Committee 1:43), implying that anyone can become an individual and that the opportunity to realize the American dream is equally open to anyone—Orrin Hatch or Clarence Thomas. By extension, the exceptional nature of the world's greatest political system is beyond dispute because only in America are justice, equal opportunity, and neutrality universally accessible.

In the Thomas hearings, we were shown a wonderful fit between individual and national virtue: worthy individuals can seize the rich opportunities that make up their country's greatness. Like the country, the personal success of Thomas and Hatch is a consequence of individual virtue, not of race/gender structures. Senator Hatch portrayed himself and Thomas as fellow Horatio Algers. Through strength of character, each managed to overcome inconvenient obstacles, and each made use of the opportunities their great country offers to those who make an effort.

Somehow, the unpaved streets, the poverty, and the Jim Crow era, all cited by Hatch, were excluded from the essence of the great country. Thomas's opening statement reassured his listeners that this was so. He referred to his early experiences in Pin Point, Georgia, as "a life far removed in space and time from this room, this day and this moment" (Committee 1:108). The mythic qualities of this story he and the Senators collaboratively narrated were already evident. Placing "this room," the Senate hearing room, in its immediate geographic location, Washington, D.C., would have instantly shrunk the distance from Pin Point. When some of the committee members were elected to Congress, Washington, D.C., including its government buildings, was a segregated city. The city currently has neighborhoods in which its children are deeply affected by poverty and race/gender domination. Many of the children's circumstances are scarcely less desperate and deprived than those of Thomas and his brother; they may be even more hopeless.

Nonetheless, Thomas reassured his eager listeners that America is about promise and those able to envision and seize it. Failures to do so, he suggested, are consequences of inadequate virtue and vision; they are not the effects of dominant relations or unequal distributions of opportunity and power. He implied that the abstract individual operates within an equally abstract political context, and race/gender relations and histories do not matter. Thomas encapsulated these contradictions when he said, "We have to remember that even though the Constitution is color blind, our society is not" (Committee 1:250).

Thomas played out and upon this fantasy in the mythic narrative he constructed about his grandfather. His constant reference to his grandfather, not his grandparents or each equally, illustrates the inextricable interweaving and operation of race/gender. The word "grandfather" had a distinct resonance for his fourteen white/male listeners that "grandparents" would not have had. The narrative construction of Thomas's grandfather served many functions throughout the hearing. First was his function as a proto-individual; he prepared Thomas to attain full individuality. Next, the grandfather served as a transitional figure in Thomas's story. His grandfather's experience was marked and limited due to his historical period, but Thomas's did not need to be. This shift in fortune over one generation is further evidence of American greatness. Rejecting Thomas's nomination would have rendered his grandfather's suffering meaningless and purposeless. It would have suggested the politically unthinkable—

that despite its promise, not everyone can redeem the American dream.

According to this story, individual virtue and structural constraints are completely independent. Thomas reminded his listeners of the "crucible of unfairness" in which their sense of justice was molded: "I watched as my grandfather was called 'boy.' I watched as my grandmother suffered the indignity of being denied the use of a bathroom" (Committee 1:109). Despite his lack of opportunities for public expression. Thomas's grandfather never abandoned his adherence to the highest moral standards. Although living in an environment of "blatant segregation and overt discrimination," his grandparents never lost their virtue. Despite the "terrible contradictions in our country," they remained "fair, decent, good people" (Committee 1:109). These behaviors and attributes rendered Thomas's grandfather worthy of the respect due to all true men (individuals). His perseverance and determination are proof that individual character ultimately determines people's fate.

Through the story of his grandfather, Thomas also situated himself within a masculinity familiar and comforting to his white/male interlocutors. Senator Spector, for example, said, "As I have read about the instructions and guidance which you got from your grandfather, I could not help but think that your grandfather and my father would have been good friends" (Committee 1:70).

Thomas's grandfather's unyielding loyalty to the highest moral standards, despite social constraints and devaluation, positioned him as fully masculine in his virtues and behavior. His perseverance through adversity and social humiliation provided evidence of his thorough mastery of one of those masculine virtues—independence, a quality Thomas later claimed for himself. In a speech Thomas gave in 1987 to the Pacific Research Institute, he made explicit these connections among masculinity, virtue, and individualism.

> The attack on wealth is really an attack on the means to acquire wealth: hard work, intelligence, and purposefulness. And that is an attack on people like my grandfather. This was a man who possessed in essence all the means of acquiring wealth a person could need. *He* could not be attacked; but the "rich" and their caricatures are easy

targets. These critics of "the rich" really do mean to destroy people like my grandfather and declare his manliness to be foolishness and wasted effort. (Committee 1:158)

Sharing this race/gender understanding, he and the senators celebrated the importance of paternal and fraternal power. Men without paternal mentors and models are likely to end up with the "terrible, terrible fate" of the men boarding buses to prison outside of Thomas's C Street office (Committee 1:260, 480). As Thomas put it,

> You know, I used to ask myself how could my grandfather care about us when he was such as hard man sometimes. But you know, in the final analysis, I found that he is the one who helped us the most because he told the truth, and he tried to help us help ourselves. And he was honest and straightforward with us, as opposed to pampering us, and prepared us for difficult problems that would confront us. (Committee 1:380)

Thomas did not state directly what he and his listeners knew. Given the demographics of Washington, D.C., and its prison population, the men with the "terrible, terrible fate" are undoubtedly predominantly young black/males.

At the end of the first hearing, Thomas commended the committee for its "courtesy and fairness" and said he had been "honored, deeply honored" to participate in it (Committee 1:520). "Only in America," he continued, could the virtue and hard lessons of his grandfather be so spectacularly redeemed. The social/sexual contract had been successfully reenacted, its promise ratified and fulfilled.

HORATIO ALGER AND BOOKER T. WASHINGTON: CONSTRUCTING "CLARENCE THOMAS"

In his opening statement, Clarence Thomas firmly located himself in a shared, familial (paternal), masculine context. After introducing Thomas's family, Chairman Biden and Thomas exchanged jokes about the relationships of fathers and sons, whether they look alike or appreciate the resemblance. Thomas described himself as a loving father and husband. He stated that much had been written about him and his family during the previous ten weeks; however, he said, "Through all that has happened throughout our lives and through all adversity, we have grown closer and our love for each other has grown stronger and deeper" (Committee 1:108). Thomas stated his "deep gratitude" to Senator Danforth and expressed his appreciation for Danforth's "wise counsel and his example over the years" (Committee 1:108). It is difficult not to read a race/gender subtext into these remarks. Thomas presented himself as a good son bidding for full initiation into elder, paternal status. Danforth played the role of Thomas's proud father, mentor, and sponsor.

Thomas laid claim to such status on the basis of his character: "I hope these hearings will help show more clearly who this person Clarence Thomas is and what really makes me tick" (Committee 1:108). This curious phrasing about himself recurred throughout Thomas's testimony. He spoke of himself as if he were an external other, objectively possessed and recounted ("this person Clarence Thomas"). In the same sentence, he described himself as a site of subjective experience ("what really makes me tick"). This language reflects a major defense Thomas used in his self-representation—splitting. He frequently distinguished between himself as "me" and as "this person," giving them different roles. "Me" was Thomas's experienced and owned subjectivity. It remained constant through many role changes. He assumed and discarded roles without affecting his essential subjectivity. Thomas was able to disavow responsibility for the positions and writings arising out of his roles while claiming full credit for the "me," his personal virtue. Political positions are a function of roles, but virtue is an expression of innate character.

Although splitting is a common psychological defense, it also reflects the operation of race/gender. Despite Thomas's intention to represent himself as an abstract individual, this defense reflects the effects on subordinates of race/gender arrangements. As DuBois discussed, for their survival, subordinates must acquire a "double consciousness."[1] It is not safe for subordinates to rely on their own subjective beliefs and desires. They must learn to see themselves as the dominant imagine them. The fantasies of the dominant exert enormous influence on the lives of the subordinate. Therefore, the capacity to experience aspects of subjectivity as an alien other—to make the subject an object—becomes a powerful aspect of subordinates' conscious and unconscious process. In a hostile world, splitting is a survival tool. It protects one against both real and imagined dangers.

Thomas's life-narrative took the form of a morality tale. It was told as the story of a character formed by circumstances. These circumstances both developed particular virtues and validated his claim to them. From the beginning, Thomas staked out both his exceptionalism and his ordinary normality. As a result of both, he suggested, he had a right to be included in the dominant relations of power. He began this narrative as though he were a therapy patient, discussing his "earliest memories." These are of the childhood in Pin Point, Georgia, of "a life far removed in space and time from this room, this day and this moment. . . It was a world so vastly different from all this" (Committee 1:108). Immediately after evoking a life so far removed from the present (and, by implication, the experience of his listeners), he described himself and his brother as young Huck Finns, catching minnows and skipping shells across the water. A scene of tremendous suffering and deprivation, bravely endured, followed this pastoral interlude. In 1955, his brother and mother went to live in Savannah; they occupied one room in a tenement. They shared a kitchen with the other tenants and a "common bathroom in the backyard which was unworkable and unusable" (Committee 1:108). Despite such deprivation, Thomas did not indulge in self-pity. He described his experience objectively and almost impersonally: "It was hard, but it was all we had and all there was" (Committee 1:108).

His grandparents rescued him from this abject poverty. His mother had been a maid and earned only twenty dollars every two weeks. So, later in 1955, she arranged for her sons to live with their grandparents. Thomas told a heart-wrenching story of arriving with his brother at their grandparents' home. "Imagine, if you will, two little boys with all their belongings in two grocery bags" (Committee 1:108). Such suffering, however, warranted no entitlement, Thomas insisted. Instead, Thomas launched into a series of environments where hard work and high expectations were the norm. At home, his grandparents taught him by example that "hard work and strong values can make for a better life" (Committee 1:108). He told the committee that he wished his grandparents were alive to see that "all their efforts, their hard work were not in vain" (Committee 1:108). His nomination redeemed and justified their sacrifices and faith. He had attended a segregated, parochial school, where the nuns were equally demanding—unyielding in their expectations that we use all our talents no matter what the rest of the world said or did" (Committee 1:108). Thomas had eagerly assumed this responsibility and attended a seminary, Holy Cross College, and Yale Law School.

So far the story had been of individual effort and self-reliance. Thomas then incorporated a more public context—the civil rights movement. He had implied personal benefit from the movement when he discussed attending Yale. The school had "opened its doors, its heart, its conscience, to recruit and admit minority students" (Committee 1:108). As he did throughout his testimony, however, he insisted that he never gained an advantage based on racial preference. His achievements reflected only his abilities and his capacity to make use of the opportunities available to him. He asserted that he had "not during my adult life or during my academic career been a part of any quota" (Committee 1:251).

Thomas did acknowledge that without the efforts of civil rights leaders and organizations such as Martin Luther King and the Southern Christian Leadership Conference (SCLC), "there would be no road to travel" (Committee 1:108). The language Thomas used to describe the nature and effects of these efforts was, however, consistent with his emphasis on individual virtue. The civil rights movement "opened doors," "knocked down barriers," and made society reach out and affirmatively help. The need for such political struggles, he suggested, does not suggest flaws in the basic structure of American politics. The problem lies not in the basic structure but in that some people lack full access to its benefits. There are, he said, "so many individuals who are left out of our society who deserve and should have a central role of full participation in our society and all that it has to offer" (Committee 1:470). According to Thomas's testimony, there is no relationship between the basic operation or the nature of the political system and its persistent and extensive exclusions.

Thomas's testimony implied that the responsibility to choose one's road and one's destination remains fully individualized. In this context, too, Thomas evoked his grandfather, who taught him the hard and essential lesson. Only at this point in his testimony, when quoting his grandfather, did Thomas slip into country vernacular: "I can still hear my grandfather, 'Y'all goin' have mo' of a chance then me" (Committee 1:109). The lesson was that only those who have internalized his grandfather's lived virtues—to be fair, hard-working people who always gave back to others—can seize and make the most of these chances.

Thomas's story conveyed that he had learned and lived these lessons well. He had "always carried in my heart the world, the life, the people, the values of my youth, the values of my grandparents and my neighbors, the values of people who believed so very deeply in this country in spite of all the contradictions" (Committee 1:110). Their sacrifice, he suggested, imposes an obligation on those who follow: "to work hard, to be decent citizens, to be fair and good people" (Committee 1:109). Thomas told the committee that he hoped it would conclude that he too is an "honest, decent, fair person" (Committee 1:111). His possession of such virtues rendered him trustworthy and credible (Committee 1:296, 324) and qualified him to be a justice:

> I believe that the obligations and responsibilities of a judge, in essence, involve just such basic values. A judge must be fair and impartial. A judge must not bring to his job, to the court, the baggage of preconceived notions, of ideology, and certainly not an agenda, and the judge must get the decision right. Because when all is said and done, the little guy, the average person, the people of Pin Point, the real people of America, will be affected not only by what we as judges do, but by the way we do our jobs. (Committee 1:111)

Thomas used race/gender discourse in both subtle and overt ways throughout the first hearing. Not only did Thomas have a right to inclusion, he implied, but his practice of such virtues entitled him to a position of moral and political superiority on race/gender matters. His testimony illuminated how even those oppressed by race/gender arrangements are invested in them and extract power from them. The dominated can deploy their position as a source of power, expertise, and control. Simultaneously, they can claim their history as warrant for universal rights and inclusion.

For example, Thomas insisted that he would not take any ideological baggage with him to the Court. He would, however, "carry with me the values of my heritage: fairness, integrity, open-mindedness, honesty and hard work" (Committee 1:111). The word "heritage" reveals Thomas's strategy in manipulating race/gender relations and meanings in representing himself. The reference to his heritage was double edged. With this word, Thomas made himself both integral to and a victim of American history. He intended to evoke both respect and deference rooted in guilt. The values of his heritage are identical to general American ones and, by enumerating them, Thomas asserted his right to be included the American dream. The implication is that his family's (and race's) adherence to and practice of these virtues despite terrible conditions marked them as super-Americans. Despite the failures of white people to practice their own values, blacks remained moral and loyal citizens; Thomas's grandfather practiced what his oppressors merely preached, and such loyalty deserved high reward.

Referring to the history of domination and to his own race/gender expertise was a means to silence the senators and immunize himself from question or criticism. Thomas evoked white guilt to control his interrogation. Even in the first hearing, Thomas did not hesitate to use the "race card." He employed it when the senators questioning became uncomfortable or revealed contradictions between his prior political stances and current testimony. There are two particularly striking and recurrent examples of this tactic. Thomas faced frequent and rather hostile questioning from liberal Democrats concerning some of his writings and speeches. These apparently endorsed a particular conservative version of natural law philosophy. To blunt or deflect such criticism, Thomas portrayed himself as a Lincoln-esque figure, describing himself contemplating slavery, civil rights, and the most effective way to appeal to the conscience of others. He also justified his support of conservative writers who advocate elevating the level of constitutional protection for property rights. Thomas claimed his motivation was a deep desire to find ways to defend the hard work of people like his grandfather. Thomas frequently made statements like this one:

> Senator, as I noted, my interest particularly in this area of natural rights was as a part-time political theorist at EEOC [the Equal Employment Opportunity Commission] who was looking for a way to unify and strengthen the whole effort to enforce our civil rights laws, as well as questions, to answer questions about slavery and to answer questions about people like my grandfather being denied opportunities. Those were important questions for me. (Committee 1:168; see also Committee 1:191)

Thomas consistently used race/gender themes to distance himself from his earlier advocacy of conservative constructions of natural law. He was especially eager to disavow the implications they held for property rights, social welfare policies, and abortion. Instead, he portrayed himself as a brave independent who simply utilized such writings to confront conservatives with the need for more aggressive support of civil rights:

> My point was that I figured or I concluded that conservatives would be skeptical about the notion of natural law, but one of their own had endorsed it, and I simply wanted to give some authenticity to my approach, so that I could then move on and get them to consider being more aggressive on the issue of civil rights. That was very, very important to me. (Committee 1:147)

Of course, it is dangerous to stake out a specific race/gender position. Thomas claimed the moral high ground of race/gender history. In addition, he simultaneously rejected and needed to transcend the social construction of black masculinity. If he had represented himself within his apparent race/gender position. Thomas would have taken on the taint of stereotypical black masculinity. Black/males are characterized as irrational, hypersexual, violent, antisocial, dangerous, physically powerful but mentally deficient, unrestrained, and enraged. These attributes form the menacing other, the opposite of the heroic, self-disciplined grandfather. The prisoners Thomas could see from his office are believed to embody (literally) these negative qualities. Thomas needed to convince his listeners that he had truly escaped their terrible fate. Equally important, he had to persuade his listeners that he would not take advantage of his admission into full power. He would never enact vengeance on them (white/males) for the suffering of his race/gender kin. On the contrary, Thomas assured his listeners that his commitment to fairness would, in fact, increase his sensitivity to the rights of all, including by implication, white/males:

> Judge Thomas: I think that we have to do as much as possible to include members of my race, minorities, women, anyone who is excluded into our society. I believe that. I have always believed that, and I have worked to achieve that.
> Senator Spector: What is the best way to do it?
> Judge Thomas: And that is the question, how best to do it. I think that you have a tension, you want to do that and, at the same time, you don't want to discriminate against others. You want to be fair: at the same time you want to affirmatively include and there is a real tension there. I wrestled with that tension and I think others wrestled with that tension. The line I drew said that we shouldn't have preferences or goals or timetables or quotas. I drew that line personally, as a policy matter, argued that, advocated that for reasons I thought were important. (Committee 1:234–235)

Thomas somehow needed to allay common white anxieties and fantasies about black masculinity. Because black/males are perceived to be deficient by dominant standards, to warrant full entry into the world of masculine/individual, Thomas needed to erase his race/gender position. He needed to become "this person," Clarence Thomas. "This person" did not possess the qualities stereotypically attributed to black/males. Even Senator Thurmond commended him for his judicial temperament, which included the "self-discipline to base decision on logic, not emotion" (Committee 1:23). Throughout the first hearing, Thomas repeatedly described himself in the language of restraint, hard work, self-discipline, and control. Often he characterized himself as open minded, fair, and decent. By implication, reason—not passion or instict—governs him. He insisted he had mastered the crucial lessons of his profession. Thomas's testimony suggested that his judicial philosophy matches his temperament, that he welcomes the restraint of precedent and legal reason and rejects an activist view of the court. Furthermore, his testimony implied, this judicial temperament is much more comfortable to him, as he prefers judicious deliberation to the rough debate and ideological burdens that dominate the political and policy arenas.

Thomas reassured his listeners that he was not angry: "I think that anyone who grew up where I grew up, in the world that I grew up in, would be deeply impassioned about civil rights enforcement. But I was trying to engage not only the passion but the intellect" (Committee 1:191). As he matured, he explained, he put aside earlier militant attitudes in a commitment to the search for unity and consensus. He told the senators that he had grown "older, wiser, but no less concerned about the same problems" (Committee 1:370). Thomas expressed his frustration that reasoned debate on civil rights approaches never took place: Rather than "ultimately sitting down and beginning to work out the problems, we were spending our time yelling across the table at each other" (Committee 1:449). "I have also, even in the heat of debate, attempted to talk reason, even though I, like perhaps everyone else, was susceptible to the rhetoric in that debate" (Committee 1:234).

Thomas even reconstructed the discrepancies the senators identified between his prior writings and current testimony as evidence of his rationality, open-mindedness, and fairness. He may appear to have taken a variety of conflicting positions, he suggested, but these differences are simply a function of his changing roles and such shifts should not raise any questions about his integrity or honesty. His rational self was not formed by any of them, he explained: "I am the same person. I think the role, again the judicial philosophy versus being a policymaker, is different" (Committee 1:483). Policy positions are simply baggage he can take up or abandon as necessary:

When one becomes a judge, the role changes, the roles change. That is why it is different. You are no longer involved in making policy. You are no longer running an agency. You are no longer making policy.

You are a judge. It is hard to explain, perhaps, but you strive—rather than looking for policy positions, you strive for impartiality. You begin to strip down from those policy positions. You begin to walk away from that constant development of new policies. You have to rule on cases as an impartial judge. And I think that is the important message that I am trying to send to you; that yes, my whole record is relevant, but remember that was as a policy maker, not as a judge. (Committee 1:267; see also Committee 1:388, 483)

Thomas presented himself as the ideal Rawlsian rational delibera-tor. Like Rawls's citizens, Thomas assumed the "original position" of objectivity and neutrality. He could don the veil of ignorance by "stripping down" to his rational core before deliberating or rendering judgement. Thomas repeated this language several times, as in this passage:

Senator, I think it is important for judges not to have agendas or to have strong ideology or ideological views. That is baggage, I think, that you take to the Court or you take as a judge. It is important for us, and I believe one of the Justices, whose name I cannot recall right now, spoke about having to strip down, like a runner, to eliminate agendas, to eliminate ideologies, and when one is a judge, it is an amazing process, because that is precisely what you start doing. You start putting the speeches away, you start putting the policy state-ments away. You begin to decline forming opinions in important ar-eas that could come before your court, because you want to be stripped down like a runner. So, I have no agenda, Senator. (Commit-tee 1:203)

Thomas was claiming a privilege typically asserted by white/males: a mind/body split, with the mind unaffected by social rela-tions and historical circumstances. The mind, he suggested, can ab-stract itself from any particular race/gender or other social location, although it can consult these if necessary or useful. Thomas's race/gender position remained "other" in a double sense. It remained undisturbed by his stripping down to reason. As a rational person, he was disembodied and therefore outside any race/gender location.

His rationality, however, enabled him to take up his specific experience as a source of sensitivity or information. Experience does not taint or shape reason, he implied. Thomas and his supporters could commend his judicial temperament (objectivity, fairness, and open-mindedness). Simultaneously, they could praise the special sensitivity to matters of race and poverty rooted in his childhood experience. The potential contradiction here was elided with the word "sensitivity," which describes an emotion. The possessor of reason can observe and suspend any emotion's effects. One can have such an emotion and still produce and ensure "fairness." It was not in the senators' interest to dispute this epistemology. Disputing it would have rendered them vulnerable to inconvenient questions about their position. Their capacity to exercise neutral judgment and deliberate without prejudice might then also have been subject to challenge.

CHAPTER TWO

The Male/Africanist Presence:
Senatorial Representations

Under the "advise and consent" function it is our solemn duty to
explore any doubts about you and your thinking. The theme of this
hearing could be entitled "Doubting Thomas." The term "Doubting
Thomas" has been applied to individuals from biblical times, but it
is applied today in a different context. You are not the doubter. It is
we in the Senate who are the doubters. This hearing can remove,
clarify, increase, or decrease the doubts and the doubters.
                                          —Senator Heflin (Committee 1:68)

Thomas was not the only one to construct a narrative of himself for
strategic and political purposes. So, too, did the senators. Thomas's
nomination provides an illuminating example of how white subjects
construct and benefit from what Toni Morrison has named "the
Africanist presence."[1] The Africanist presence—Clarence Thomas in
this instance—allowed the senators to locate themselves and by extension the "America" they represent in relation to racial domination.
They could do so without appearing to have been shaped or advan-
taged by, or complicit in, it. Although the senators may have doubted
Thomas, they never put themselves in question.

Each senator either tacitly or explicitly acknowledged that Thomas
was being nominated for the "black seat" previously held by Justice
Thurgood Marshall. Marshall, the senators frequently acknowledged, was a "giant" in the history of the civil rights movement.
Eight of the senators (Biden, Grassley, Hatch, Kennedy, Leahy, Metzenbaum, Simon, and Spector) mentioned this context in their opening remarks. This was unavoidable race/gender history that could
have undermined the story America wanted to tell about itself.
Thomas's explicit race/gender positioning had the potential to disrupt the (white/male) equilibrium of the Senate hearing room. It

both permitted and required restoring networks of power and knowledge. If America were truly the land of equal opportunity and greatness celebrated by the senators, then Thomas's race/gender position would have been irrelevant. The senators handled this dilemma by emphasizing Thomas's role as the race/gender other. Thomas bore the black/male's burden of race/gender representation. White/males consider themselves fully individual and unfettered; no such task fetters or weighs on them. In the Thomas hearings, the senators demonstrated a primary function of the Africanist presence. The Africanist presence enables the dominant group to maintain its unmarked race/gender position. It renders by contrast the dominant group as external to and not responsible for relations of domination.

Despite Thomas's wish to strip down to reason and to gain full membership in the world of unmarked individuals, his race/gender was inescapable. He could not erase or elude being the marked and subordinate other. Senator Grassley obliquely acknowledged the race/gender divide:

> In the Senate we have some who have started from humble beginnings and many who were born in great wealth and privilege. None of us, however, has had to surmount the obstacles Judge Thomas confronted. Racism and prejudice from his cruel teenage classmates in the seminary to supposedly enlightened employers he encountered as a young law school graduate. (Committee 1:66)

Unlike Thomas's permanent and inescapable race/gender position, the senators were in the unusual and uncomfortable position of occupying a marked race/gender location; their position was, however, temporary and escapable. The hearings were an opportunity for them to actively represent themselves to each other, to Thomas, and to the nation. They had to describe the nation to itself, and their narrative was constructed in such a way that race/gender seemed outside of the mainstream of American history. It remained extrinsic to the personal experiences and subjectivities of its dominant groups.

A repeated theme in the senators' opening statements and through-out the first hearing was the meanings and effects of America's race/gender history. To sustain the view of American "greatness" and the "American dream" the senators represented, this material could not be directly integrated into the main story line. Race/gender could not be shown as shaping the common course of American history. To contain the potential disruptions that reworking history might cause, Thomas needed to remain the bearer and the agent, the victim and the object of race/gender. It remained a story about "them," not "us." "Us" was white people, who were the nation. It also needed to be a story with a happy ending. Whatever obstacles may have existed in the past, the story needed to relay, "they" can now overcome them and through their own individual efforts redeem the promise on which the nation was founded.

Within this safe rubric, the senators were free to indulge in ex-tended ruminations on the meanings, history, and current state of race/gender relations in America. The Africanist presence allowed the existence and effects of race/gender domination to be simultane-ously admitted and denied. It could be acknowledged as long as its focus was on its victims and especially as long as its most brutal ef-fects were in the past. Most of the views articulated by the committee members overlapped with those of Senator Kennedy:

> The civil rights revolution . . . is far from complete. Millions of our
> fellow citizens are still left out and behind because of unacceptable
> conditions of discrimination based on race, sex, age, disability, and
> other forms of bigotry that continue to plague our society. (Commit-
> tee 1:36)

Kennedy's implicit message was that this history and its contem-porary effects are located in an external other, that subjects do not practice and benefit from race/gender domination, and that bigotry is an alien illness that "plagues" the nation. These beliefs allow the dom-inant group to deny the consequences of race/gender dominance for itself—privilege and excessive power and resources. Mainstream accounts of American history can incorporate experiences of suffering by and discrimination against African Americans; however, the agents and beneficiaries of such relations remain notably absent. The senators' construction of civil rights focused on the victims, on the inequities African Americans have suffered. There was no mention of the fact that positions of privilege such as those held by the senators are at least a major part of the cause of the problem.

For the senators, Thomas's presence was an opportunity to articulate and discharge their own positions on the current state of race/gender relations. It enabled them to discuss the distribution of power and the agents responsible for any lingering inequalities. They disagreed over conclusions about America and contemporary race/gender relations they could draw from Thomas's life story, but all of the senators used Thomas to send their own message to those in disadvantaged positions. Each of these messages offered one of two morals. One was that Thomas's triumph over adversity and discrimination proved that no formal or structural barriers to equal opportunity still existed. His example should inspire those in disadvantaged positions. They can aspire, as he did, to work their way upward. Senator Simpson clearly articulated this view:

> Judge Thomas, I think you will also be very good for America on the broader level. You yourself have noted that there is some risk, obviously, that there are too many people giving groups excuses for various things that happened in their lives. I am not even going to comment on that. You can. You have. But I think the last thing anyone needs right now in this country, white, brown, yellow, or black, is more excuses for everything. Excuse time is over. It is important to run out of scapegoats. It is time for all Americans—and that is what we are in this pluralistic society—to focus again on what has made this country great, and we must all reacquaint ourselves, all of us, every race, color and creed, with those distinctly American and yes, even corny notions of hard work and decency and kindness and fairness to our fellow humans, and we must strive to provide every single individual with an equal opportunity to realize his or her full potential. You exemplify what all of us might be able to accomplish, good thing if we were to stop making excuses . . . So, you are an inspiration to us all. (Committee 1:61–62)

Senator Simpson, for example, said:

> I . . . understand your explanation of your exploration of this thing called natural law in an effort to find meaning in a Constitution that apparently permitted slavery in the United States. That must have been a most torturous path to travel, one that I nor any one of us could even conjecture. (Committee 1:192)

Why would this be so? Certainly for any American citizen, a full grasp of the meanings of the Constitution would have to include the compromises concerning slavery. These compromises, fully incorporated, made its ratification possible. The historical context of slavery has had profound meanings to, and effects on, not only those who suffered from it but also those whose ancestors benefited from it. The compromises that allowed a tolerance of slavery to be built into the document on which the American republic was founded are an intrinsic aspect of the American story. Regardless of how differently its benefits are distributed, all American subjects continue to live out its effects.

PARTIAL ACCOUNTING IN THE SENATORS' REPRESENTATIONS

This history remained unacknowledged and unexplored in the hearings. The senators offered no account of contemporary constructions of white subjects or of how past social arrangements shaped present ones. We have no account of race/gender relationships delineating their complex interactions, mutual dependence, costs, and benefits. The senators failed to consider discrimination's Siamese twin—privilege. Many effects of race/gender relations, therefore, remained invisible. These relationships continue to produce and sustain persistent, interdependent, and asymmetric distributions of power. Race/gender arrangements generate narratives through which dominant groups establish our subjectivities. White subjects can admit that "mistakes were made" but no one needs to take responsibility for their consequences in our own lives. These consequences can remain irrelevant to the contemporary distribution of respect, power, and resources. As discussed in Chapter 8, taking responsibility bears no resemblance to white liberal guilt. Such guilt deflects responsibility.

These constructions of race/gender therefore make it logical to assume that only those in subordinate positions can have any useful

Similarly, Senator Grassley said:

> He grew up without material comforts and even conveniences. We
> have heard from him and people who have known him well that it
> wasn't even until he was seven years old that he lived in a home with
> indoor plumbing. His home was run quite strictly by his grand-
> parents who, in his words, had Ph.D.s in life earned at the university
> of experience with hard times as their advisor. They instilled in him
> discipline and respect. It seems to me that discipline is a shortcoming
> in too much of American society today. So, in having that in Judge
> Thomas puts him a cut above average American society. (Committee
> 1:66)

Senator Kohl succinctly tied these themes together: "Yours, indeed, i
the story we want to tell about America in the 20th century. It testifie
to our achievements in creating opportunity for all from a social con
tract written for just a few" (Committee 1:80).

Other senators were more restrained in their claims, and offered
second moral. They used Thomas's story as a cautionary tale abou
the benefits of affirmative action. His story revealed the incomplete
ness of struggles against America's racial past. Without the existence
of affirmative civil rights policies, they postulated, Thomas may no
have been able to attend Yale Law School and fulfill his promise. His
success was used to demonstrate the need for an activist governmen
and renewed dedication to social welfare policies.

No one, however, considered what the senators could have learned
about current power arrangements by taking seriously the race/
gender composition of the committee itself. Just as Jim Crow laws
were extrinsic to the meaning of American history, so too the intimate knowledge of race was foreign to these white/male senators
Senator Hatch even called racial bigotry "un-American" (Committee
1:42). The underlying assumption was that the lives of white people
are not equally affected by their own race/gender positions. Oppression was understood solely in terms of the (more or less past) experiences of African Americans and the unacceptable conditions
they suffered. The opposite but interdependent condition of oppression—privilege—was strangely absent in the historical narrative.

The Male/Africanist Presence: Senatorial Representations

knowledge of race/gender. Understanding how race/gender works is not part of "ordinary" experience, and so subordinated persons bear the burden of introducing this alien knowledge into the dominant system. Their "normal" (excluded/inferior) position is reversed. They are accorded an automatic competence in this limited (and delimiting) area of specialization. As in Myrdal's much earlier account,[2] the American dilemma remains the black/male's burden. Regarding privilege, furthermore, "special sensitivity" evidently does not exist as dominance does not generate its own forms of knowledge.

When white subjects appeared in the senatorial narratives, it was only as the new victims of "reverse discrimination." Senator Hatch, for example, asserted:

> Now, just as our society had finally enacted long overdue laws to prohibit racial, ethnic and gender discrimination, new forms of discrimination were invented, ostensibly in the name of civil rights. Innocent persons were made new victims of discrimination as a purported means of remedying discrimination against others and as a redress for a history these new victims had not created. (Committee 1:42)

Someone must make "innocent persons" victims of discrimination, he implied. Yet, those who benefit from the victimization of African Americans remain unidentified. Only civil rights zealots appear to have the power to victimize others. White/males are doubly innocent. They lack any responsibility for or benefit from American race/gender history. Instead, Senator Hatch suggested, white/males are victims of newly invented forms of discrimination—preferences for women and minorities.

This reversal is a particularly interesting use of the Africanist presence. It enables white/males to invert their positions. It reverses agency and erases past and present distributions of power. The subordinates are posited as now controlling the distribution of privilege and as being responsible for the outcomes of race/gender arrangements. A transformation in the naming of the problem emerged. "Preferences" and privileges supposedly flowed to the subordinate, not to the dominant, race/gender positions. Commitment to equality now meant protecting the rights of the privileged.

This logic is evident in the way expertise was repeatedly attributed to Thomas. This expertise supposedly came simply from his personal experience. For example, almost all of the senators' opening statements referred to his privileged knowledge of, and "special sensitivity" to, America's race/gender history. Senator Nunn said:

> Clarence Thomas has climbed many jagged mountains on the road from Pin Point, Georgia, to this Senate Judiciary Committee. I believe that if he is confirmed, Judge Thomas will remember his own climb and will always insist on fairness and equal justice under law for those who are still climbing. (Committee 1:84)

Senator Danforth asserted, "Everyone in the Senate knows something about the legal issues before the Supreme Court. Not a single member of the Senate knows what Clarence Thomas knows about being poor and black in America" (Committee 1:97).

Not all of the senators were convinced that Thomas would discharge the burden of his position satisfactorily. The more liberal senators agreed with Kennedy that Thomas "deserves great credit for the eminence he has attained" (Committee 1:36). Despite this, Metzenbaum insisted, the question for the committee was "not where does Judge Thomas come from, rather the question for the committee is this: Where would a Justice Thomas take the Supreme Court?" (Committee 1:63). On this issue, he remained quite uneasy:

> There are those who suggest that because of his extraordinary background, Judge Thomas will bring a different perspective to the Court. That may be true. It also may not be true. I am concerned that the nominee's statement and record indicate that, rather than bring a different perspective to the Court, he will fit in all too well with the Court that has spurned its special duty to protect the rights of women and minorities, the elderly, and the poor. (Committee 1:63)

Thus, at least implicity, the determining relationship between race/gender and political positions is questionable. Do any "special sensitivities" necessarily follow from a particular racial position and socioeconomic background? Opinions remained divided. Although some senators may have accorded such privilege to Thomas, they were not willing to apply the same logic to themselves. Those in privileged positions would seemingly be affected. They would reveal an absence of sensitivity to others. They would create an (at least unconscious) interest in maintaining their privilege and superiority. They would be biased on race/gender matters. This logic seems to support the need some senators articulated for "diversity" on the Supreme Court. They specified diversity as one reason for backing Thomas. To counteract the effects of such race/gender privilege would require special efforts, and these preferences could compensate for the effects of past unfairness and current consequences. The senators themselves would have to endorse race/gender preferences. They would actively seek out diversity, which could counteract and correct their own limits, positions, prejudices, and errors.

This, however, was not their view, which instead was that race/gender locations shape only *subordinate* subjects. No senator considered how he might have benefited from longstanding preferences for white/males. Nonetheless, the senators repeatedly asked Thomas to acknowledge his debts to civil rights movements and legislation. White people are not constructed as bearing an obligation to give back in exchange all of their years of benefiting from race/gender preferences. Thomas's questioners felt comfortable challenging Thomas to account for how he was discharging his debt to his own community and to the nation. Some continued to doubt whether he would be a worthy successor to Justice Marshall in carrying out this task. Unlike the senators, however, Thomas could not escape the burden of the race/gender other. It is not difficult to understand why Thomas would have wanted to manipulate this burden to his own advantage. The best he could hope for was to evoke some of the guilt that often lies under professions of innocence and good faith. Appeals to guilt, however, have their limits. They frequently evoke a counterproductive backlash. The senators, like many white subjects, depended on and deployed the Africanist presence to reaffirm their moral purity in race/gender matters. They comfortably positioned themselves as fair-minded advocates of equal opportunity and as dedicated protectors of the weak and underprivileged. Several represented themselves as resolutely race/gender blind. They specify that their commitment was not to race/gender favoritism for anyone, oppressed or powerful, but to equality.

Some demonstrated this deep commitment by championing the rights of women. The senators repeatedly questioned Thomas about privacy rights, abortion, and *Roe v. Wade.* This positioning as protectors of women and the rights of all later haunted the senators when they were confronted in the second hearing with Anita Hill's charges. They were then unable to escape taking her charges of sexual harassment seriously, or at least of appearing to consider them.

SETTLING THE DEAL: USING THE PARADOXES
OF RACE/GENDER

Throughout the first hearing, Thomas and the Judiciary Committee struggled with the limits and logic of liberal ideas and practices. They considered the contradictory meanings of American history. Talking about the history of race/gender relations was, however, destabilizing. It was threatening even though they attempted to contain its extent and effects. Throughout the hearings, the senators often referred to race/gender arrangements through the safer code of black people's experience with segregation in the South. This language made "the South" acquire an alien location, as if it were a foreign place outside of America. They projected race/gender oppression onto this mythic location, allowing it to appear extrinsic to America. This attempted splitting, was not however, completely successful. Discrimination, even if in less malevolent forms, appeared to exist outside of the South. Acknowledging it disrupted narratives of America's special goodness, white people's innocence, abstract individualism, and the neutrality of law and political institutions. The meaning of domination for American politics was at stake. The hearings confronted the senators, Thomas, and the American audience with some of our most urgent and troublesome political questions. What was the current status of race/gender relations? What was the appropriate way to understand them, both now and in the past? The senators disagreed on the extent to which race/gender still affected people's life chances and what "equal opportunity" afforded. To what extent were individuals' current positions the consequence only of virtue and character? How would people be ranked in power and respect when race/gender no longer had any lingering effect?

Although the participants in the hearing disagreed on such issues, they did not question the language with which to consider them: the individual was the basic unit of society. The problem of race/gender was understood within the rubric of inclusion and exclusion. Inclusion was possible by demonstrating individual worth. We display worth through such virtues as decency, discipline, and hard work. This approach allowed no possibility of questioning the identity or the worthiness of the judges or of the capacity of the evaluating processes to make such "fair" decisions. The dominant narrative stipulates that the social context is representative and fair.

The senators were nonetheless compelled to grapple with the paradoxes of "diversity." How do we handle difference, they were forced to ask themselves, if we believe that the abstract individual is the basic unit of the political world? The system is supposed to be open to all (equal opportunity). The only way to verify this openness is to observe the particular characteristics of those who are included. Such observation requires recognizing "difference" within the system. Yet, within a system of equal opportunity, difference must disappear. Once admitted into competition, each subject's race/gender becomes irrelevant, and the outcome is not affected by particular differences. It is determined only by worth, which presumably exists independent of all particular race/gender differences. Worth is supposed to be determined objectively, and this evaluation has nothing to do with particular characteristics. Once difference is included, it is ignored. Inclusion in turn ensures that the "best" will be chosen; it warrants the fairness of the process. It is simply assumed that, like the free market, the chooser and the process are rational, although the need to ensure diversity suggests that this is now always the case. Outcomes persistently skewed along race/gender line suggest problems of individual worth or error, not the fairness of the process.

Thinking about race/gender as structural rather than individual threatens the rationality of the system. If race/gender is structural, it is not simply a matter of individual attitudes or conscious choice. Moreover, structural processes such as law or administration cannot be assumed to be neutral as the unconscious bias of those in power will taint them. To test the fairness of the system, we would then have to look at outcomes, which is one reason that "quotas" and "affirmative action" are troubling. Raising the problem of "preferences"—who benefits from them and who is disadvantaged—suggests that the process itself is tainted. The chooser's bias would subvert rational choice. Such claims undermine the separation between rational process and social context, which is a formative and essential aspect of abstract individualism.

Thomas was useful to the senators. He enabled them to finesse the tensions among race/gender, difference, and equality. He affirmed the plausibility of abstract individualism. He encouraged their belief in the essential fairness of the system, meaning that anyone can become like them. His own ideology meshed with theirs, and his appointment to the Supreme Court would be further evidence of this "truth." If a poor child from segregated Pin Point, Georgia, can become a Supreme Court Justice, then they can claim that the credibility of the American dream is indisputable.

Many senators made comments similar to those of Senator Brown, a Republican from Colorado.

> Clarence Thomas brings to the Court an understanding of segregation as one who has felt its oppression. He brings to the Court an understanding of poverty as one who has experienced it firsthand. And I believe he brings to the Court an understanding of the American dream as one who has lived it. (Committee 1:77)

In other words, Thomas's presence before them proved that the system was race/gender neutral regarding individuals. It neither permitted a black/male to obtain this position nor impeded him from doing so.

Simultaneously, however, Thomas and the senators needed to agree that Thomas's race/gender identity had consequences. Otherwise, his nomination would not have signaled a commitment to diversity. It could not have proved the openness of competition within the system. His conservative views raised doubts about his race/gender identity. How can a black man from Pin Point, Georgia, be a Reagan Republican? At one point, in a fascinating dialogue between Senator

Simon and Clarence Thomas, Simon explicitly articulated these assumptions:

> Anyway I see these two Clarence Thomases. One who has some extremely conservative and I would even say insensitive—maybe you wouldn't agree with that description—and then I hear the Clarence Thomas with a heart. And Senator Heflin says you are in part an enigma, and that is part of the enigma. How do I put these two Clarence Thomases together, and which is the real Clarence Thomas? (Committee 1:380)

Thomas answered, "Senator, that is all part of me" (Committee 1:380).

Thomas adopted a variety of strategies to ease anxieties about his identity. He called on a shared liberal belief in the neutrality of law and judicial processes. He reminded the senators that in taking up a judicial position one assumes a new "objectivity," one that erased the previous political ideas and commitments some find so troubling. Several times he made statements such as the following:

> I think it is important that when one becomes a member of the judiciary that one ceases to accumulate strong viewpoints, and rather begins to, as I noted earlier, strip down as a runner and to maintain and secure that level of impartiality and objectivity necessary for judging cases. (Committee 1:226)

Yet, Thomas reassured the senators, his "stripping down" would not strip away his special sensitivities. Although his prior political commitments have been stripped away, these sensitivities endured and he would remain a "race man." Sensitivity was an expression of his character, not of his roles. These contradictions were wonderfully enunciated in a dialogue between Senator Kohl and Thomas. Kohl asked Thomas why he wanted to be a Supreme Court justice. Thomas replied,

> It is an opportunity to serve, to give back. That has been something that has been important to me. And I believe, Senator, that I can make a contribution, that I can bring something different to the Court, that I

can walk in the shoes of the people who are affected by what the Court does . . . on my current court, I have occasion to look out the window that faces C Street, and there are converted buses that bring in the criminal defendants to our criminal justice system, busload after busload. And you look out, and you say to yourself, and I say to myself almost every day, But for the grace of God, there go I. (Committee 1:260)

Kohl replied,

Judge Thomas, if I understand you correctly, you are going to leave behind almost all of your views about what type of society we ought to be and what type of policies we ought to apply. Two questions. First, why after 20 years in the forefront of these battles do you want to leave all of this behind? And the second question is: If you leave so much of this behind, what is left? (Committee 1:260)

Thomas answered that he did not miss the battles of the political process, that he preferred the reasoned debate of the court. Thomas then made an extraordinary statement about what was left:

But with respect to the underlying concerns and feelings about people being left out, about our society not addressing all the problems of people, I have those concerns. I will take those to the grave with me. I am concerned about the kids on those buses I told you. I am concerned about the kids who didn't have the strong grandfather and strong grandparents to help them out of what I would consider a terrible, terrible fate. But you carry that feeling with you. You carry that strength with you. I don't think you have to carry the battles with you. It is a difficult weight. (Committee 1:260)

Once fully admitted into the world of abstract individuals, his statement implied, the weight of race/gender would lift. Some of the senators, however, voiced a different hope. Like many political leaders of subordinate groups, some senators believed that eventually Thomas's experience would have its "normal," reasonably expected effect. When Thomas became a Supreme Court justice, they hoped, he would show the special sensitivity to minorities that people "like" him are supposed to share. Would subordination "in the last instance" determine his judicial philosophy? Several senators stressed their belief that it would. Despite contrary evidence in his writings and public activities, they expected that in his new position Thomas would be particularly sensitive to the needs and conditions of the less powerful. He would assume Marshall's role on the court as the protector of those who had not yet full realized the American dream. For example, Senator DeConcini seemed to assume this:

> Judge, the reason I raise this here is that if you are confirmed and you become Justice, you would have, in my judgment, based on your background, your educational background, your family background and who you are, every reason to have a greater sensitivity than anybody here. (Committee 1:327)

Despite this emphasis on special experiences and sensitivities, the senators could not confirm Thomas's appointment on race/gender grounds. Thomas's nomination could not appear to fill a quota. Appointment on these grounds would violate an ideology Thomas and the senators shared, namely that quotas violate the principles of individualism and equal opportunity. They admit marked persons into the system *because of their difference.* In neither processes nor outcomes could race/gender be irrelevant. This would clearly violate the liberal notion of an individual who can and must function as disembodied possessor of rights. The senators needed to evaluate Thomas as an unmarked "individual." The only appropriate criteria were those of merit: he was the best person for the job, not the best black/male President Bush could nominate to the court. In this context, his insistence that "I have not during my adult life or during my academic career been a part of any quota" (Committee 1:251) was necessary and understandable.

Thomas's race/gender was noted only to be publicly disregarded. The relevance of race/gender to his inclusion, but its irrelevance to his success, proved that the system was simultaneously diverse and race/gender blind. His conservative views discomforted some but they also were reassuring. He would not disturb the system. Unlike

Marshall, who wrote increasingly bitter decisions denouncing racial domination within the law and the blindness of his fellow justices to it, Thomas would not challenge the fundamental fairness of American law and political processes. Thomas assured the senators that while he was committed to civil rights, he was not like the prisoners on the bus. He was not one of those frightening, angry black/males who would make them uncomfortable. He spoke of creating a "comfort level" for conservatives on racial issues:

> And I thought that we should advance the ball, that the issue of race has to be solved in this country and we have to stop criticizing each other and calling each other names. And I was involved in that debate, and I was a pretty tough debater, too. But at some point we have got to solve those problems out here. (Committee 1:243)

As a justice, he conveyed, he would remain loyal to the principles of the Constitution despite or because of his special experiences and sensitivities. His confirmation affirmed the intrinsic justice of the system. He himself was not angry and would not call its constituting practices into question. The system simply needed to include more people like him within it.

With hard work, even a poor boy from Pin Point, Georgia, could grow up to be a Supreme Court justice. This message was compelling for what it said about Thomas and, equally important, for what it said about the contemporary American political system. To reject his nomination would have been to undermine the story "we" want to tell about America. The investment in this narrative was so strong it overrode or occluded other concerns, including questions about Thomas's lack of judicial experience, his past policy positions, his "vanishing views," and his repeatedly inconsistent testimony to the committee. Senator Metzenbaum summarized the many inconsistencies in Thomas's testimony:

> Instead of explaining your views, though, you actually ran from them and disavowed them. Now, in a 1989 article in the *Harvard Journal of Law and Public Policy*, you wrote, "The higher law background of the American Constitution, whether explicitly appealed to or not, pro-

vides the only firm basis for just, wise and constitutional decisions". But yesterday you said, "I don't see a role for the use of natural law in constitutional adjudication. My interest was purely in the context of political theory."

Then in 1987, in a speech to the ABA, you said, "Economic rights are as protected as any other rights in the Constitution." But yesterday you said, "The Supreme Court cases that decided that economic rights have lesser protection were correctly decided."

In 1987, in a speech to the Heritage Foundation, you said, "Lewis Lehrman's diatribe against the right to choose was a splendid example of applying natural law." But yesterday you said, "I disagree with the article, and I did not endorse it before."

In 1987, you signed on to a White House working group report that criticized as "fatally flawed," a whole line of cases concerned with the right to privacy. But yesterday you said you never read the controversial and highly publicized report, and that you believe the Constitution protects the very right the report criticizes.

In all your 150-plus speeches and dozens of articles, your only reference to a right to privacy was to criticize a constitutional argument in support of that right. Yesterday you said there is a right to privacy. (Committee 1:178; see also Senator Kennedy, Committee 1:444; Senator Spector, Committee 1:494)

Thomas also responded inconsistently to questions about constitutional issues and Supreme Court decisions. He discussed his views of some Fourteenth Amendment and right-to-privacy cases in great detail (Committee 1:360–365); yet he insisted he had no opinion on *Roe v. Wade*. He maintained he had never talked about it with anyone, even though it was decided while he was in law school.

Thomas was as invested in the mainstream narrative about America as the senators were. Within the context of the mutually agreed upon account of the American dream, his character defense made sense. It made full use of the powerful narrative of abstract individualism:

But those conclusions that people form about you were not—about me were not the real Clarence Thomas. I am the real Clarence

Thomas, and I have attempted to bring that person here and to show you who he was, not just snippets from speeches or snippets from articles. The person you see is Clarence Thomas. I don't know that I would call myself an enigma. I am just Clarence Thomas. And I have tried to be fair and tried to be what I said in my opening statement. And I try to do what my grandfather said, stand up for what I believe in. There has been that measure of independence.

But, by and large, the point is that I am just simply different from what people have painted me to be. And the person you have before you today is the person who was in those army fatigues, combat boots, who has grown older, wiser, but no less concerned about the same problems. (Committee 1:370)

The legitimacy of the political system, including the Senate, was at risk during the Thomas hearings. If the nominee could not attain the status of an abstract individual, then "this person" Clarence Thomas would remain a subordinate other, mired "all the way down" in his race/gender position. He and others in his position would remain imprisoned in an oppressive America, unable to acquire the power accorded individuals in the system. He would have been unable to escape the dominant other's need to construct him as inferior. The race/gender innocence of the senators and the American political system would have been in question. In thanking the senators for "the fairness and the courtesy that you have shown me through this process" (Committee 1:521), Thomas signaled his belief that he had escaped the terrible fate. His faith in the American dream remained intact; he had finally ascended. Soon he would "be able to put his feet under the bench in the highest court in this land, as he contemplates the finer points of the law" (Committee 1:43). Everyone present wanted to believe and confirm his closing statement: "Only in America could this have been possible" (Committee 1:521).

CHAPTER THREE

The Female / Africanist Presence: Male Bonding in Contemporary American Politics

Two tales are told of sores no salve can cure;
Hear now the third and worst,
Where marriage harbours hate,
Where woman's brain can plot
Fierce treachery against her warrior mate.
Whose brow his trembling enemies saw
Darkened with majesty and awe—
There stands a house by all gods accursed!
Honour belongs where home and hearth are pure,
Where neither hate grows hot,
Nor woman's daring impulse reaches
Beyond the bound that virtue teaches.[1]

Clarence Thomas encountered an interruption in his progress toward putting his feet under the Supreme Court bench. Following the first hearings, someone leaked Anita Hill's charges of sexual misconduct. A second round of hearings was held exactly one month later, in October 1991. The narrative established in the first hearing made Hill's charges potentially devastating. The committee members all agreed that Thomas's capacity to overcome adversity was evidence of extraordinary merit and that his virtue made him a commendable candidate for the job. Challenges to his character would have undermined his qualifications, calling the committee's judgment and objectivity into question. If the committee could not accurately identify merit, citizens might wonder, how can other elements of the political system be presumed fair? The plausibility of equal opportunity rested on the belief that merit is objectively identifiable and that the system distributes rewards solely on this basis.

Had Thomas and the committee constructed a different narrative, their reaction to Hill might not have been so fierce. Within their linguistically negotiated space, there was no room for any force that would reintroduce race/gender as constraining, dominating, structuring, particularizing, or delimiting. At best, race/gender positions are enabling and positive. As one strips away or leaves behind their particulars, they provide experience that sensitizes and builds character. (Past) victimization or oppression generates ethical commitment. Having been a victim means one will never victimize others.

An effective way out of this bind was to erase Anita Hill. The committee's loyalty to dominant institutions and their legitimating narratives required it to treat Hill and Thomas very differently. Hill's treatment would be the exact opposite of Thomas's. Through narrative, the committee transmuted Thomas into an abstract individual. It incorporated him into the bounds of dominant race/gender power. Hill, however, never escaped her preexisting race/gender position, the female/Africanist presence. Hill could not be incorporated as a truth-telling, virtuous subject within the dominant narrative of race/gender power. The coherence and plausibility of the narrative required her expulsion.

From the beginning of her testimony, Hill—not Thomas—was the subject of doubt. To take her narrative and charges seriously would have suggested that the political system is not exactly the way the first hearing portrayed it. The committee and Thomas had agreed that it is imperfect but still exceptional and that abstract individualism and equal opportunity can be achieved. Hill's story suggested that sexual exploitation is a privilege of and means to exercise and maintain power. In contrast, by supporting Thomas, the senators reaffirmed that the system "works" and it is what it is said to be. Thomas's story reinforced a view of power without race/gender domination; the plausibility of Hill's story required admission of such domination. Erasing Hill as a serious political subject allowed the positive narrative to remain undisturbed and intact.

Hill's charges provided a common object against which male bonding and solidarity rallied. Unlike Thomas, Hill did not succeed in constructing a self-defined space as a subject in the hearings. She remained an object, with her representation shaped by the others' projections and the functions she had to perform in order for dominant narratives to retain coherence and efficacy. Interactions between the senators and Hill provided a public example of how the denigration of female subjects is essential to the construction of male ones. The process of constructing male subjects is complicated by tensions in race/gender relations, potential conflicts between race/gender loyalties, and requirements to rise above these loyalties. The language used to construct Hill in the interactions by and among Judiciary Committee members was particularly revealing. The senators unwillingly illustrated the race/gender specificity of the Africanist presence as they used Hill to represent themselves. Hill, in constructing herself, did the same. These interactions revealed a great deal not only about race/gender but also about the unequal distribution of political power and narrative resources in contemporary American politics.

The second hearing was so startling in part because it exposed normally denied, displaced, or depoliticized material and relationships. Rarely do subjects so publicly acknowledge the interrelationships among masculinity and the possession, protection (paternalism), and control of women. These processes are usually subtle and ongoing and frequently involve transactions that on their surface have no overt relationship to race/gender. They are often enacted through language and significant absences or silences—for example, the failure of men to intervene in others' oppressive behavior. An example is the "benign neglect" or tolerance of workplace and political cultures that are hostile to women. These cultures encourage at least temporary alliances among men across class and race positions. These alliances are both sources and expressions of power. In the hearings, however, these usually hidden mechanisms appeared. The usual boundaries between public and private that are intrinsic to liberal politics, including bureaucratic rationality and sexual behavior, visibly broke down at both individual and structural levels.

Without this veneer, the ordinary range of responses to threats against race/gender power became visible. Exposure of ordinarily hidden circuits threatened to generate a crisis of legitimacy. To return to stability, disrupted and exposed networks had to be repaired and hidden. The second hearing accomplished this through the denigration and erasure of woman to effect male bonding and social construction of masculinities. Hill's position as the female/Africanist presence determined the particular form of the traditional process. This hearing was a public reenactment of the race/gender contract that courses through modern liberal political institutions.

ANITA HILL'S STORY: FURY OR RELUCTANT WITNESS?

Thomas's heroic character had been the dominant narrative throughout the first hearing. In the second hearing, however, despite its potential for a similarly sympathetic construction, neither Hill nor the senators approached her life story in the same way. The senators did not praise Hill for her efforts, character, virtue, or contributions to the authenticating and fulfilling the American dream. They did not accord her space for self-construction or the authority to determine the plot lines. Instead, Hill and the senators struggled for narrative control. They confronted conflicting storylines: Was Hill a passive participant whose integrity and privacy had been violated? Or was she an active agent who had chosen to channel thwarted ambition, zealous political beliefs, or frustrated sexual desire into a scheme to destroy a good man?

The structure of Hill's account of her relations with Thomas directly paralleled her story about how she came to testify. Hill represented herself in both situations as a modest woman whose privacy had been transgressed. Some senators immediately rejected her presentation because modesty and privacy are not qualities associated with a black/female. The senators immediately questioned Hill's credibility, motives, and character. Senator Biden insisted that the subject of the hearing be exclusively the truth of Anita Hill's account of Thomas's behavior toward her. The only relevant question before the committee, he insisted, was the credibility of two people (Committee 4:101). Despite their repeated distinctions between a trial and a hearing, the senators made it clear that the burden of proof rested on Hill. Thomas had to be considered innocent until he was proven otherwise, and Hill had to remove any shadow of doubt (Committee 4:188–189).

The senators quickly reframed their questions about motivation. They focused on Hill's motives for making (or making up) her changes. They searched for motives to lie, and they evinced little curiosity about her motivations to tell the truth. Spector accused Hill of "flat-out perjury" (Committee 4:230), and Simpson reported,

And now, I really am getting stuff over the transom about Professor Hill. I have got letters hanging out from my pockets. I have got statements from her former law professors, statements from people that know her, statements from Tulsa, Oklahoma saying watch out for this woman. But nobody has the guts to say that because it gets all tangled up in this sexual harassment crap. (Committee 4:253)

The senators constructed Hill in contradictory forms. She was an aggressive quasi-male expert capable of exploiting her knowledge and power to protect herself and achieve her ends. Alternatively or simultaneously, she was a passionate woman determined to get her man through seduction or revenge. From the beginning, there was sexual resonance in the senators' language and representations. A frequent line of questioning was how Hill's charges became public. The senators' questions often had sexual connotations, with terms such as "initiate contact" and "withdrawal." The relevance of this line of questioning was puzzling until it became clear that the real issue was Hill's virtue. It is assumed that only the innocent can be violated. Like any woman making a charge against a man, Hill's credibility depended on the establishment of prior virtue.

Establishing credibility was impossible for Hill. Although she refused to play on her race/gender position, she was undone by it. Because of the dominant race/gender arrangements, she, a black/female, could not claim modesty, virtue, or the protection of dominant males. She was vulnerable to the ugliest consequences of her race/gender and became the object of sexual fantasies, shaming, humiliation, and contempt. Simultaneously, she was made the agent and the cause of this treatment. Even if Hill was truthful in her charges against Thomas, the senators could not acknowledge Thomas's guilt. To maintain race/gender relations, they had to engage in and replicate their earlier behaviors.

In her opening statement, Hill mentioned a few biographical facts. She is the thirteenth child of an Oklahoma farming family. Like

Thomas's Hill's childhood youth, "was the childhood of both work and poverty (Committee 4:41). She was nurtured by her family's support and deep religious faith. Her membership in the Baptist church was "a very warm part of my life at the present time" (Committee 4:36). Despite poverty, Hill went to college and then to Yale Law School. She then worked for a private law firm. At age twenty-five, she went to work at the Office of Civil Rights in the Department of Education as attorney-advisor to Clarence Thomas.

Beyond the charges of sexual harassment, there were striking differences between Hill's and Thomas's accounts of each other. Hill did not portray herself as the ward of a responsible, paternal, mentoring figure. She did not view Thomas as a friend, a member of her family, or a reliable source of counsel or support. Instead, she presented herself as having been torn between conflicting desires to engage in civil rights work and to elude an unpredictable harasser. Hill said,

> Well, I think it is very difficult to understand, Senator, and in hindsight it is even difficult for me to understand, but I have to take the situation as it existed at that time. At that time staying seemed the only reasonable choice. At that time, staying was the way that—in a way, a choice that I made because I wanted to do the work. I in fact believed that I could make that choice to do the work, and that is what I wanted to do, and I did not want to let that kind of behavior control my choices. (Committee 4:122–123)

If Hill experienced any frustrated desire, it arose from this conflict, not from sexual attraction to Thomas, thwarted ambition, or a wish to be his favored employee. Contrary to Thomas's and Doggett's view of her, Hill said that she had not been lonely, inept, or sexually frustrated; she had had a "normal social life with other men outside the office" (Committee 4:42). Hill said that she experienced relief—not envy or frustration—when she moved on to the Equal Employment Opportunity Commission (EEOC); the staff grew, and her contact with Thomas diminished (Committee 4:45–48) Hill had no wish to be promoted within the EEOC, for that would have meant more contact with Thomas.

According to Hill, Thomas's sexual harassment began at the Department of Education, after Hill had been working there for approximately three months. The harassment tapered off four or five months later. Following a few month's respite, she said, Thomas began harassing her again; this was at the EEOC during the fall and winter of 1982 (Committee 4:109). Hill said that Thomas asked her five to ten times to go on dates with him. She said that she made it clear each time that she had no interest in dating him. She alleged that Thomas engaged in sexual conversations with her, both in his office and in the cafeteria. These conversations included descriptions of pornographic movies, including women with large breasts, men with big penises, and sex with animals. She said that she indicated that she did not wish to engage in such conversation and that she tried to steer their discussion to other topics. She said that Thomas also discussed his own sexual endowment and prowess, including special skill in performing oral sex. On one occasion at the EEOC, she said, Thomas was drinking a Coke while she was working with him in his office. She said that he "got up from the table at which we were working, went over to his desk to get the Coke, looked at the can, and said, "Who has put pubic hair on my Coke?" (Committee 4:45). She claimed to have repressed many of these details. She retained clear memory of some of Thomas's statements, and others were recalled under the senators' repeated questioning (Committee 4:66, 76).

Hill said that by late 1982 she was experiencing severe stress in her job. She had assumed that Thomas was pressuring her for sex, although he had not demanded it. Hill believed that Thomas enjoyed her vulnerability and wanted her under his control, sexually or otherwise. She also believed that he would use his power to accomplish this goal (Committee 4:88–89). Hill was afraid that Thomas would retaliate for her rejection of his overtures. Although she did not take notes about his behavior at the time, she did document her work. If she had been fired, she said, she could have proved her competence and professionalism (Committee 4:79). Hill's concern was not to prepare for litigation against Thomas, but to protect herself (Committee 4:80). Hill's primary goal was to stop Thomas's harassment so that she could continue her work (Committee 4:86).

In January of 1983, despite Hill's commitment to civil rights work, she began to look for another job. She felt an increasingly desperate need to escape what was becoming an intolerable situation. In February of 1983, she was hospitalized for five days with stomach pain with an unidentified cause; she attributed this pain to stress. At that time, Hill discussed feeling stressed with at least two friends but she did not disclose the details of its cause. Following her hospitalization, Hill intensified her job search and sought to minimize further her contact with Thomas. Avoiding Thomas, not a wish to return to Oklahoma or to teach, was her primary motive in seeking another job. She was pleased when Thomas appointed an office director because most of her interactions were with the director. Contact with Thomas was generally limited to staff meetings. In July of 1983, Hill left Washington, D.C., and had minimal contact with Thomas after her departure. Most contact concerned professional matters, such as obtaining references or arranging conferences.

When the senators asked why Hill had not reported Thomas's behavior at the time that it occurred and why she later maintained a relationship with him, Hill provided several reasons. The structure of the race/gender arrangements made none of Hill's explanations particularly plausible or comprehensible to the senators. Most of the senators quickly rejected her explanations. While citing Thomas's legal expertise in sexual harassment policy as evidence of his innocence, the senators used Hill's position against her. As a professional and a lawyer, they suggested, Hill would have been motivated to sue, not to elude her tormentor. Hill responded that she was not an expert in sexual harassment (Committee 4:80). At the time of the hearings, approximately eight years after Thomas had harassed her, she said she felt less threatened and more hurt and angry than she had. Then, she had felt humiliated, embarrassed, and ashamed, and had sought to control Thomas's behavior with cautious and discreet deflection. She had been reluctant to "cut off all ties or to burn all bridges or treat him in a hostile manner" (Committee 4:83) because she had believed that she "could not afford to antagonize a person in such a high position" (Committee 4:105).

It is unlikely that the senators could understand the pressure on women to take responsibility for men's sexual behavior toward them. Failure of a woman to control a man's sexual behavior suggests a deficiency or lack of virtue in the woman, not the man. It is understood that it is in men's nature to behave in a sexually forward manner and that real women ward off their advances, are so chaste and unexciting that they do not interest men, or deserve what they get. Modesty is a means for women to maintain self-regard and social respectability. Women can control men's behavior only with discretion, withdrawal, diversion, and avoidance. Open aggression in a woman is suspicious because it suggests lack of self-control and excessive passion, including sexual desire. A woman who is unable to control a man's sexual behavior feels ashamed. To avoid being socially disgraced, she handles her shame internally and does not complain.

These pressures to take responsibility for men's sexual behavior are more intense for black/females than for white/females. Black/females are often stereotyped as particularly "loose," aggressive, and sexually provocative. The senators sympathized with Thomas's complaint that he was being dirtied by stereotypes about black/males, but neither Hill nor the senators discussed stereotypes about black/females. Much of Hill's language about shame, embarrassment, and humiliation remained a code. The senators were unable or unwilling to grasp the complex messages of the code.

Hill persistently represented herself as a reluctant, modest witness. In demeanor and language, she presented herself as someone who responded to outside forces rather than initiated action. She was not the seducer but the transgressed, not active but passive, and not aggressive but reluctantly responsive. Subliminally she attempted to ward off the stereotypes of unashamed, hypersexual black/females. Because she is a modest woman, however, Hill did not, perhaps could not, attack these views directly. Although she frequently represented herself as passive, Hill did not characterize herself as a victim. Unlike Thomas, she made no explicit use of her race/gender position; instead, she presented herself as a servant of truth with an obligation to tell it. Once Hill's privacy had been breached, her duty was to offer the committee information. She could not tell the committee what the information meant or what should be done with her disclosures.

Hill's self-representations resemble the feminine virtues stereotypically possessed by white/females. According to stereotype, a good woman tries to maintain control by withdrawal or discretion. She is reluctant to use aggression on her own behalf, and, even in crucial matters such as employment, she relies on advice or information from male superiors. Similarly, Hill's entire self-representation can be summarized in one statement she made: her "desire was never to get to this point. The desire—and I thought that I could do things and if I were cautious enough and I could control it so that it would not get to this point, but I was mistaken (Committee 4:87). Hill's language is revealing. She couched even her own desire for privacy in the passive voice. She did not represent herself as exercising agency on her behalf or as being a desiring subject. She portrayed herself as a cautious servant of "the desire" for discretion and control.

In keeping with the themes of modesty and virtue, Hill presented herself as a reluctant witness, insisting that she had not initiated contact with the committee. At each stage in the process, she had been the seduced, not the seductress. Had committee staffers not approached her, she would never have come forward. Had her statement not been leaked, she would not have spoken publicly. She said that she had "had no intention of being here today, none at all. I did not think that this would ever—I had not even imagined that this would occur (Committee 4:86). Ultimately, she said her love for truth forced her to act. After leaks to the press, she was compelled against her wishes to speak publicly. Her purpose was then to eliminate rumors and to tell the truth (Committee 4:132). She said, "I felt I had a duty to report . . . [there was] no other choice but to tell the truth" (Committee 4:48).

Hill insisted that she had no "personal vendetta against Clarence Thomas" (Committee 4:48). This statement signaled that she was neither an aggressor nor a conspirator in, or an instrument of, a plot to destroy Thomas. Although she disagreed with aspects of his philosophy, she said, she was not a zealot who would use any means to achieve her ends (Committee 4:132–133; 135). Hill did not believe that simply putting forward her allegations would cause Thomas to withdraw (Committee 4:118); in fact, she had nothing to gain by testifying (Committee 4:116).

Despite Hill's reluctance to testify, she did not represent herself, as Thomas did, as a victim of the process. Furthermore, unlike Thomas, Hill could not attack the committee. Doing so would have further marked her as aggressive and discredited her "femininity." Hill did not accuse anyone of making her testify publicly or of disrupting her life. She saw the obligation to testify as "just the reality of situation" (Committee 4:121).

In her opening statement, Hill represented herself as a moral agent and as someone who made choices that may be flawed and imperfect:

> I may have used poor judgment early on in my relationship with this issue. I was aware, however, that telling at any point in my career could adversely affect my future career. . . . As I said, I may have used poor judgment. Perhaps I should have taken angry or even militant steps, both when I was in the agency or after I had left it, but I must confess to the world that the course I took seemed the better, as well as the easier approach. (Committee 4:39–40)

In this refusal of victimization, Hill shut off one possible source of empathy from the senators. To have gained their empathy, she could have tried to evoke pity, guilt, or sympathy. Hill had already positioned herself as a flawed and conflicted person, a stance that undermined her credibility and made establishment of a recognizable identity even more difficult.

In basing her credibility on truth, Hill confronted the constraints of race/gender arrangements. She needed to prove her moral worthiness and veracity before she could be trusted. In the second hearing, the senators replaced the thematic question of the first hearing, "Who is the real Clarence Thomas?" with a new one—"Who is the real Anita Hill?" As Senator Heflin stated, "We are still left with a quandary as to where we are. And as I stated in the first hearing, what is the real Clarence Thomas like? I think an issue now is what is the real Anita Hill like? And we have to make the decisions relative to those issues" (Committee 4:241).

Hill was unable to answer this question satisfactorily. She could not establish the right to be heard. Her failure was inevitable, given the limits of the race/gender arrangements. Within the senators' understandings of identity and history, there were no positive places for them to situate her. Black/females are never Horatio Algers. Their history of sexual vulnerability and exploitation cannot be a source of empathy for white/males. Instead their presence implicates white/

males in black/female subordination. To protect white/males from complicity in the subordination of black/females, the behaviors and beliefs developed by black/females to resist and transform stereotypes must remain incomprehensible to white/males. The senators could not understand why a black/woman might feel humiliated by sexual harassment and paralyzed by shame. Nor could they understand why she might blame herself rather than publicly accuse a man of wrongdoing. Senator Leahy provided an example of this incomprehension when he asked if Thomas ever stopped Hill from leaving his office, as through intimidation and domination require physical force. Leahy's question also resembles the traditional approach to a woman's claim of having been raped. To acquire any credibility, women must provide evidence of physical force (Committee 4:75). In addition, the senators could not understand a black/woman's sympathy for the vulnerability of a black/male in a white/male world. The intense pressures on black/females to stand behind their men, often coded as "race" loyalty, were incomprehensible to the senators. They could not comprehend the possible effects on Hill of persistent accusations of black/female "disloyalty." Black females frequently face accusations of undermining "their men" or of betraying them to whites in the pursuit of their own interests.

The senators questioned Hill's credibility because she admitted that she had sought to maintain cordial contact with Thomas (Committee 4:83). The senators could not believe that if harassment had occurred, Hill would have followed Thomas from the Department of Education to the EEOC. If she had been harassed, she would not have maintained "cordial" relations much less worked with him. For the senators to have comprehended such behavior would have required actively imagining a subordinate's race/gender domination. For Hill's narrative to have been plausible, the senators would have had to imagined the powerlessness, isolation, and marginality intrinsic to Hill's position as a black/female (as well as a Republican and a professional). It is unlikely that Hill would have encountered many persons who shared her race/gender position or who felt an obligation to ensure her well-being. Hill undoubtedly had a powerful need for allies, mentors, and role models. Instead of imaging Hill's position, the senators discounted her narrative. If Thomas had overcome isolation and powerlessness, they decided, so could Hill.

Although none of the senators exhibited any comprehension of Hill's self-representation or its historical context, some committee members actively rejected her representation. They constructed Hill as both a lawyer/expert and a vengeful/irrational woman bent on undoing a good man. She had failed to be sufficiently active or passive. As a lawyer, she would have occupied a position of equality with Thomas (and the senators), and placing her in a parallel position, they can imagine that she is just like them. Therefore, she would have been knowledgeable and powerful enough to resist "harassment." Spector articulated this view twice, at the beginning and end of her testimony:

> The testimony that you described here today depicts a circumstance where the Chairman of the EEOC is blatant, as you describe it, and my question is: Understanding the fact that you are 25 and that you are shortly out of law school and the pressures that exist in the world—and I know about it to a fair extent. I used to be a district attorney and I know about sexual harassment and discrimination against women and I think I have some sensitivity on it—but even considering all of that, given your own expert standing and the fact that here you have the chief law enforcement officer of the country on this subject and the whole purpose of the civil right law is being perverted right in the office of the the Chairman with one of his own female subordinates, what went through your mind, if anything, on whether you ought to come forward at that stage? If you had, you would have stopped this man from being head of the EEOC perhaps for another decade. What went on in your mind? I know you decided not to make a complaint, but did you give that any consideration, and if so, how could you allow this kind of reprehensible conduct to go on right in the headquarters, without doing something about it? (Committee 4:68; see also Committee 4:134)

Spector's statement was typical of many of the committee members' responses. They presented themselves as sympathetic to women and knowledgeable about the dynamics of sexual harassment. Their short-lived sympathy for Hill and her position as a young, vulnerable woman was undercut immediately by focusing on her as a lawyer. She was denied the condition of a victim and is instead characterized as professional who is derelict in discharging her duty. She was no longer considered a "woman," a person vulnerable to harassment but came to be viewed as an abstract, disembodied "expert." Such "experts" are perceived to be dominant, not subordinate. They are believed to have sufficient authority and knowledge to control any potential harasser and to bring the force of the law against him. The senators questioned Hill's credibility because she did not take notes on Thomas's behavior when he supposedly harassed her. As a lawyer, she must have known that notes would have made her charges more credible and so the lack of notes proves that the alleged behavior did not occur (Committee 4:70). Even if Thomas had harassed her, the senators imply, Hill—not Thomas—was wrong because, given her position as a professional, she should never have allowed the harassment to continue. Any deserving person would understand her obligation to use her power and position to enforce the law.

The senators did not have to imagine what it might be like to be a young, black professional woman. They could not imagine how imperiled one's place might feel in a professional environment. It is reasonable to assume that the senators themselves were unlikely to face limited choices or to feel dependent on the whims of other men. Rarely are they confronted with a choice between self-respect and continuing to do work they love (or even sheer survival). Nor can they imagine the effects of race/gender training that encourage women to believe that their relationships matter more than anything else. This training encourages women to believe that the way to succeed is to establish and maintain good relationships with others, especially with men. These relationships have become women's definition of success.

Furthermore, the senators do not want to imaginatively identify with Hill. Despite eagerly positioning themselves as the victims of Hill's harassment, committee members are also reassuring each other of their own race/position. It would be too subjectively threatening for them to imagine a situation in which their power was insufficient to exercise control. Their willingness to imagine Hill's position was further limited by their belief that real males are not sexually vulnerable and that power protects them against exploitation, including its sexual forms. Race/gender solidarity requires men to respect each other's integrity and, as subordinates, females cannot aggress against the dominant. Even if the senators somehow found themselves in the dilemma Hill described, surely they would and could use the force of the law to protect themselves.

So, instead of imagining Hill's position, they question Hill's motives for moving with Thomas to the EEOC. They discounted her explanation that she was afraid of losing her job at the Department of Education because it might have been abolished or, if it remained, a new head might have wanted his own staffperson in the position. The senators could not imagine that Hill might have been unaware that she had been a schedule A employee and entitled to job security. They also could not believe that she would not have inquired about her job status. They would never simply take their boss's word that there might not be a job for them (Committee 4:99).

The senators also questioned Hill's state of mind. They used eleven calls to Thomas over seven years against her. These calls are characterized as evidence of her "repeated efforts" to contact him. If Thomas really had harassed her, they asked, why would she ever call him again (Committee 4:128)?

The senators' questions projected their own feelings of entitlement. They faulted Hill for not acting in accordance with expectations that arise out of their own privileged sense of place. They used her to disavow their own fears of losing such privilege or of being unable to control their own fate. By identifying with Thomas and rejecting Hill's explanations, they reassert the power of individual virtue. Hill's self-described failure to find a satisfactory way to assert control ratified her lack of virtue. The senators would never find themselves in her position, limited to unwanted choices and conditions. Real individuals (men) either avoid such adversity or use it as an opportunity to display their transformative powers, prowess, and worth.

Hill had no grounds for solidarity with her fourteen white male questioners. She was neither a mother nor a wife, and, unlike Thomas, Hill had no male sponsor or protector. Toward the end of the second hearing, Senator Kennedy protested her treatment by members of the committee:

I hope we are not going to hear a lot more comments about fantasy stories picked out of books and law cases. . . or how there have been attempts in the eleventh hour to derail this nomination. I hope we can clear this room of the dirt and innuendo, that has been suggested by Professor Hill as well, about over-the-transom information, about faxes, about proclivities. We heard a good deal about character assassination yesterday, and I hope we are going to be sensitive to the attempts of character assassination on Professor Hill. They are unworthy. They are unworthy. And, quite frankly, I hope we are not going to hear a lot more about racism as we consider this nominee. The fact is that these points of sexual harassment are made by an Afro-American against an Afro-American. The issue isn't discrimination and racism. It is about sexual harassment, and I hope we can keep our eye on that particular issue. (Committee 4:307–308)

Despite Kennedy's sympathy toward Hill, he missed the complex interaction of gendered aspects of racial subordination and racial aspects of sexual harassment and gender dominance. Despite Kennedy's protests and occasional sympathethic interventions by Senators Biden and Metzenbaum, when necessary the committee erased Hill's race/gender position. She was transformed from the female/Africanist presence into an archetypical hysterical spinster. The committee characterized Hill as an intensely ambitious, selfish female whose lack of success with men rendered her vengeful and prone to fantasy. Her race/gender position undoubtedly affected her treatment, too. She did not benefit from the usual obscuring veneer of male "chivalry," "protection," or "respect" bestowed on some heterosexual white/females. White/males are willing to come to the defense of some (white) women as long as doing so does not dislodge their own privilege. Race/gender norms require white/males to offer paternal protection to family members. White/males are expected to extend courtesy to females who they can imagine as wives or daughters.

The second hearing was dominated by a systematic and rhetorical assault by some senators and their allies on Hill's motives, integrity, and even her sanity. By attributing certain characteristics to her, some senators deemed her as undeserving of paternal protection. Traditionally, charges of rape were considered inapplicable to black/females; so, too, Hill was placed outside of the class of sexually harassable women. Some senators go even further. They transformed Hill into a castrating harpy. She is portrayed as exploiting her powers of sexuality and vengeance, either acting on her own or, as many black/females have done, allowing herself to be used by others as a pawn to destroy a black/male (Committee 4:424). Simpson couched his accusations in vivid language:

> Because all we have heard for 103 days is about a most remarkable man, and nobody has come forward, and they scoured his every shred of life, and nobody but you and another witness, apparently who is alleging no sexual harassment, has come forward.
> And so may, may, it seems to me you didn't really intend to kill him, but you may have. And that is pretty heavy. I don't care if you are a man or a woman, to know that 43 years or 35 years of your life or 60 years of your life, where no one has corroborated what is a devastating charge, kind of a singular torpedo below the water line and he sinks, while 103 days of accumulated things never penetrated the armor. (Committee 4:128)

Like others of her ilk, Simpson implied Hill had sent her phallic charge below the belt, attempting to kill her prey by targeting and penetrating the one chink in his otherwise powerful armor.

Ostensibly searching for a motive, the senators speculated extensively about Anita Hill's psychology and relationships with men. Biden asserted, "Certain subjects are simply irrelevant to the issue of harassment, namely the private conduct of out-of-the-workplace relationships, and the intimate lives and practices of Judge Thomas; Professor Hill, and any other witness that comes before us" (Committee 4:3). The committee members respected these ground rules in their questioning of Thomas; however, they engaged in extensive questioning of Hill, Thomas, and other witnesses about all aspects of Hill's life. Sometimes this questioning sounded ridiculous. For example, Hill described dining with Thomas once at his insistence when she left the EEOC. According to Hill, Thomas told her that if information about his behavior "came out it could ruin his career" (Committee

4:72). Leahy then asked Hill if she had had an alcoholic beverage during that dinner.

The committee claimed it had to "plumb the depths" of Hill's credibility. In the search for truth, any line of questioning was relevant (Committee 4:101). The sexual connotations of this phrase, "plumb the depths," and that of the senators' repeated question about whether Hill wanted Thomas to withdraw [presumably from his nomination] are difficult to ignore. The differences in the ways that Hill and Thomas were treated reflect a norm of race/gender arrangements. Women have no private lives. Because they are inevitably at risk for displaying their sexualized characters in public, everything about them is subject to scrutiny. Men, however, keep their private behaviors separate from their public lives. Revealing these behaviors would humiliate, and even unman, them. It would undercut their (rational) masculinity and signify a lack of the equal treatment and respect they expect as and among men.

In their supposed pursuit of motives, the senators and hostile witnesses ascribe to Hill an almost comprehensive list of the negative stereotypes attributed to female subjects across race/gender positions. The senators and witnesses expended much effort in buttressing and elaborating on the validity of these motivations. They worked hard to construct a picture of Hill that was congruent with their perspectives. Like any female, they decided, Hill was driven by her emotions and unable to think for herself. She is prone to fight unfairly and to nurture grudges when she loses. Spector's "compromise" third position—that Hill is fantasizing—had even worse implications than charges of lying. Spector transformed Hill into an hysterical woman who did not deserve to be in a public place. This characterization is a powerful form of erasure and expulsion from the public domain.

Female irrationality took many forms in Hill's case. Heflin cataloged some of these: scorned woman, zealoting civil rights believer, civil rights militant, martyr complex, narcissistic ambition to become a hero, prone to fantasy (persistently out of reality), and overweening desire for public recognition through writing a book (Committee 4:87). Some senators claimed she was a political pawn or "a willing vessel" of a story made up by a group hostile to Thomas (Committee 4:253). Others described her as duplicitous and two-faced (Committee

4:374). An alternate explanation was that Hill's charges were a consequence of the long-smoldering rage of a woman scorned. Senator Simpson said, "I do love Shakespeare, and Shakespeare would love this. This is all Shakespeare. This is about love and hate, and cheating and distrust, and kindness and disgust, and avarice and jealousy and envy, all those things that make that remarkable bard read today" (Committee 4:255).

Some witnesses suggested that Hill's attachment to Thomas reflected not romantic interest but ambition; she hoped to benefit professionally from association with a "rising star" (Committee 4:363). Others claimed that fury stemmed from thwarted ambition, not romantic rejection, because she had long nurtured disappointment from her failure to "get a promotion under" Thomas (Committee 4:227). Perhaps Hill's narcissism had been injured when Thomas moved to the EEOC. With this move, Hill became a less important member of a much larger staff with less access to Thomas than she felt she deserved (Committee 4:354). Another claim was that Hill's intense ambition and self-interest may have motivated her in her interactions with the committee. She may have been using her testimony to advance her own agenda, becoming the "Rosa Parks of sexual harassment." One witness speculated, "The speaking engagements will come, the book, the movie" (Committee 4:385). Another allegation was that differences in "political philosophy" might have been part of the problem (Committee 4:248). Hill was a "civil rights fanatic" who had become an opponent of Thomas and would stop at nothing to block his appointment to the Supreme Court. She may have been mentally unstable or prone to "transference" (Committee 4:385) or fantasy (Committee 4:227). Hill was lying said another, but not intentionally—she simply could not distinguish between her fantasies and reality (Committee 4:385; 4:570). Perhaps she was acting out of jealousy or she was infatuated with Thomas (Committee 4:354–356). Her calls to him stopped when he remarried, supporting this last suggestion (Committee 4:374). Possibly she felt concern or anger that Thomas had been "dating a woman who was of a lighter complexion" (Committee 4:264).

It was predictable that whether or not Anita Hill testified, she would not be heard. Her charges put the committee in a double bind.

If the charges had been leaked to the public and the committee had failed to consider them, the committee would have appeared insensitive or biased. In order to prove the committee's "fairness" (neutrality) and to shore up its legitimacy (and that of the larger system), the committee had to provide a forum for Hill to speak. The members needed to appear to take both Hill and issues of sexual harassment seriously. Simultaneously however, the race/gender contract had to be covertly rescued in a way that did not implicate the committee (and, by extension, the political institutions it represented) in structured, sexualized dominance and control.

CHAPTER FOUR

Whose Hearing? Sexual Harassment
and the Female Tease

The committee defined its task as excluding any consideration of the relationship between sexual harassment and networks of power. Sexual harassment, like race/gender subordination, was not considered intrinsic to ordinary public life and was not a normal means through which to exercise power. The committee considered sexual harassment simply as a matter of individual behavior. Thus, they erased the complex interplay between sexuality and power and reduced the problem to competing narratives of individual behavior. Once located within "private" relationships, the issue was simply credibility—one individual's word against another's. Character again trumped structure in a move that set the stage for a second and complementary step: the systematic erasure of Anita Hill. She ceased to be an individual who deserved attention.

Biden succinctly described the committee's task:

> In the end, this hearing may resolve much or it may resolve little, but there are two things that cannot remain in doubt after this hearing is over: First, that the members of this committee are fair and have been fair to all witnesses; and second, that we take sexual harassment as a very serious concern in this hearing and overall. (Committee 4:4)

The committee felt pressured to prove that despite its gender/race distribution (and, by extension, that of the entire national political system), it was neutral. Simultaneously, it was sensitive to the experiences of "others." The senators were clearly aware of the broader political environment, including its pervasive race/gender tensions and grievances. The members worried about the political system's capacity to contain such conflict. The destabilizing effects that conflict related to race/gender tensions could have had on existing power relations and institutions (from which the senators benefited) were particularly troubling. Biden referred to the "gender gap" when he offered his putative apology to American women: "I do apologize to the women of America, if they got the wrong impression about how seriously I take the issue of sexual harassment (Committee 4:136).

In the sensitive context of race/gender the committee's composition (fourteen white/males) suddenly had become publicly marked. When Biden first heard allegations of sexual harassment he ordered that a Federal Bureau of Investigation (FBI) case be opened; however, he also chose to proceed with the first hearing before the case was closed. Questions have been raised about Biden's handling of the allegations. Why did the committee fail to investigate Hill's charges immediately after Biden circulated material about them? How could the committee have ignored such material? (Committee 4:130) Could their failure to act on Hill's charges indicate more than a simple instance of poor judgment? Do race/gender power relations mean that some subjects are not taken seriously?

The senators spent much time during the first hearing establishing the possibility of a correlation between certain race/gender positions and a special "sensitivity" to lingering inequalities. The dominant narrative in American politics, however, cannot acknowledge the converse—the relationships between privilege and race/gender positions. The senators believed that in relying on rules and procedures, they could still guarantee impartiality. Furthermore, as neutral agents, they trusted that they could achieve sensitivity, too:

> Perhaps 14 men sitting here today cannot understand these things fully. I know there are many people who suspect we never will understand, but fairness means doing our best to understand, no matter what we do or do not believe about the specific charges. We are going to listen as closely as we can at these hearings. (Committee 4:3)

Although the senators acknowledged that the Thomas hearings were extraordinary (Committee 4:96) and that their lines of inquiry were quite different from usual (Committee 4:92), they reassured one another about the objectivity of their procedures (Committee 4:112).

The senators positioned themselves as benign protectors. Biden, for example, insisted that "from the beginning, the interests at stake are those of Professor Hill and those of Clarence Thomas, not those of the committee" (Committee 4:96). The committee members also insisted that they were concerned for their wider audience and that they did not want to discourage women from pressing sexual harassment charges (Committee 4:228).

Biden even used his dedication to the principles of individualism to justify his decision to keep Hill's allegations secret. He said that he was dedicated to the protection of individual rights, including Hill's. Hill had not wanted to make the charges public, he said, so he had attempted to adhere to her wishes:

> I must tell you, every instinct in me in the world wanted to say to the whole Senate and to the whole world that we should have a hearing on this. But again, we tend to look at large issues and forget individuals. You were the individual in the middle of this . . . the purpose of the process is to protect the rights of individuals. (Committee 4:136–137)

From the beginning of the second hearing, the committee members insisted that despite their composition, they took sexual harassment seriously. The members repeatedly asserted their sensitivity to the existence and gravity of harassment. Individual senators (for example, Biden [Committee 4:2], Kennedy [Committee 4:118], Metzenbaum [Committee 4:119], DeConcini [Committee 4:120], Kohl [Committee 4:131], and Simpson [Committee 4:253]) affirmed its importance as a national issue and their commitment to fighting it. DeConcini, for example, recounted a recent dinner with his mother when she discussed experiencing sexual harassment sixty years ago:

> I just remember, as a young boy, my mother telling me about sexual harassment on her job and losing her job when she was 22 years old. So I grew up with that in my mind. She mentioned it several times as I grew in age.
>
> I had dinner with her night before last and she got choked up, just telling me again about it 60 years later.

So, it is a subject that is very sensitive. Obviously, men have a more difficult time, I believe, of understanding it, but I do believe that there are many men in this Senate, in the House of Representatives and other political offices that indeed are sensitive as much as a man can be. (Committee 4:120)

At the end of Hill's testimony, the senators thanked her for performing a "public service." Each committee member stated that Hill's testimony had made the nation and the ninety-eight men in the Senate more aware of sexual harassment (Committee 4:118–131). Simpson, for example, expressed his surprise, for he had believed that existing procedures for combating sexual harassment worked (Committee 4:324). Some senators positioned themselves as concerned fathers, thinking of their daughters' futures. They claimed that sexual harassment persisted in part because "women tolerate it," and they expressed hope that after watching the hearing, more women would feel emboldened to press charges (Committee 4:122).

To have truly taken sexual harassment seriously, the committee would have had to consider how sexual harassment is endemic to public life. Presumably, a significant number of men (and some women) are perpetrators. Otherwise, sexual harassment could not be as widespread a problem as the committee members affirmed that it is. It cannot be simply a "woman's problem," although women may be its predominant targets. Many men must observe it, tolerate it, or engage in it themselves, meaning that sexual harassment cannot be totally alien to ordinary masculine experience or simply a consequence of a bad character or a misguided attitude. Even Thomas's female supporters, as well as Hill's witnesses (Committee 4:312) and Thomas himself (Committee 4:194), testified about their own experiences of sexual harassment and its frequency (Committee 4:568–590). When one witness was pressed by committee members to affirm the efficacy of current law, she insisted that women's working conditions were not significantly different from those prevalent ten years earlier. Many women, including most of the committee's witnesses, who had experienced harassment did not pursue formal remedies. They often felt embarrassed or ashamed, feared retaliation, or assumed action would be equally painful or futile (Committee 4:323).

It would have been deeply unsettling if the senators had defined sexual harassment as a widespread model of the relationships between men and women, tolerated or supported by other social and political forces. Such a model did not fit with the narrative of equality in that it suggested that race/gender relations might be distinct forms of power within mainstream institutions. The committee could not have escaped that conclusion; therefore, it treated sexual harassment as though it existed outside of the ordinary structures of public life. The senators managed to define it as an exclusively private, female problem.

Public life included Thomas's hearings. As Biden repeatedly stated, the hearing was not supposed to be a "forum on sexual harassment" (Committee 4:119). Much "expert" knowledge existed concerning the usual responses and behaviors of people who experienced sexual harassment; however, this knowledge was not considered relevant for the hearings (Committee 4:85). No testimony was allowed about the frequency or varieties of sexual harassment or the typical reactions of harassed individuals:

> Let me make clear this is not, I emphasize, this is not a hearing about the extent and nature of sexual harassment in America. That question is for a different sort of meeting of this or any other committee. This is a hearing convened for a specific purpose, to air specific allegations against one specific individual, allegations which may be true or may not be true. Whichever may be the case, this hearing has not been convened to investigate the widespread problem, and it is indisputably widespread, the widespread problem of sexual harassment in this country. . . . This is a fact-finding hearing, and our purpose is to help our colleagues in the U.S. Senate determine whether Judge Thomas should be confirmed to the Supreme Court. (Committee 4:2; see also Committee 4:211)

Biden distinguished two separate issues: whether Anita Hill was harassed and the general pattern of sexual harassment. Only the first issue was relevant to this hearing, he said. Thus, when it was to Hill's disadvantage, Hill was positioned as an abstract individual. She was simply "one specific individual" making an allegation against another. This separation of the issues removed from the allegations all structural context. It was Hill's integrity against Thomas's. Unlike Thomas, Hill could not use a narrative of (past) oppression to underwrite her credibility and bolster sympathy. The committee deemed irrelevant similar experiences of other young or professional black/females. Simultaneously, however, they used social context against Hill. They frequently asked her why her behavior had deviated from what is expected of "normal" harassment victims.

The defining question was individual veracity: her word against his. As Heflin declared,

> I and I suppose every member of the committee, have to come down to the ultimate question of who is telling the truth. My experience as a lawyer and judge is that you listen to all the testimony and then you try to determine the motivation for the one that is not telling the truth.
>
> Now, trying to determine whether you are telling falsehoods or not, I have to determine what your motivation might be. (Committee 4:87)

This definition was not neutral; it put Hill at a disadvantage in at least three ways. The entire burden of proof rested on her. To prove her case, she first had to prove her credibility, character, and moral worth. She could not call on, name, or position herself within relevant networks of power, which foreclosed the possibility that her word would be believed.

SEXUALITY AND THE OBSCURE SUBJECT OF DESIRE

Thomas's alleged behavior explicitly connected sexuality and power in a way that could have undermined the legitimacy of the sexual contract. Part of what was at stake during the hearings was the race/gendered nature of power. Existing race/gender arrangements required both enacting and denying race/gender specific power. Hill portrayed sexuality as a weapon inappropriately deployed in the public world; however, contrary to the usual narrative, its user was a man. She identified race/gender construction and struggle within the political world. Furthermore, she labeled race/gender relationships and sexuality as forms of power and power relations as race/gendered.

How were the senators to minimize these potentially undermining claims? One way was to suggest that sexuality in the public sphere is an unfortunate and dangerous consequence of female fantasy. Race/gender solidarity required the committee (fourteen white/males) to project pathological sexuality onto women and the female imagination. Black/females, as hypersexual beings, are particularly vulnerable to such pathology, the committee members implied. Hatch, for example, suggested that Hill borrowed some of her allegations from *The Exorcist* (Committee 4:206) or an Oklahoma sexual harassment case (Committee 4:204). To the extent that Thomas had already been admitted into the brotherhood of men, Hill's charges compromised them all. To preserve masculine sexual innocence, the committee needed to attack stereotypes of black/male sexuality. They denied the possibility that the material Hill related could reflect aspects of "normal" masculinity (or fantasy life).

Hill's female/Africanist presence provided an opportunity for the senators to construct stories about "normal" male sexuality for themselves and the public. These stories reassured them and their audience that Hill, not Thomas, was responsible for the introduction of pornography, sexual filth, and perversion. Normal male behavior and fantasy lay outside of her disturbed imagination, they implied. A few perverted males may engage in such filth, but the normal and the perverted have nothing in common. The sick deviant tells us nothing about healthy, normal behavior. Deviant and normal are defined, fixed, homogeneous identities. One cannot be sexually deviant and otherwise normal. Thomas could not have been simultaneously virtuous and "perverted."

Thomas's alleged behavior was "bizarre" and "pathological," according to the senators. It was outside of the range of ordinary masculine conduct. The senators assigned the alleged pornographic behavior to Hill's unstable black/female mind. They pathologized Hill's charges and removed them from ordinary masculine possibility. Such pathological behavior is, they said, a likely expression of "mental illness" suffered by very sick men—and ordinary women. Hatch said,

But if you have all of those cumulatively together, the person who would do something like that, over a period of time, really a short period of time, according to her, and in two different separate agencies, we will put it that way, that person, it seems to me, would not be a normal person. That person, it seems to me, would be a psychopathic sex fiend or a pervert. (Committee 4:200)

Such behavior was "garbage" and alien to ordinary public life, they said. Merely discussing these behaviors was polluting or compromising:

Judge Thomas: Senator, I think this whole affair is sick.
    Senator Hatch: I think it is sick, too.
    Judge Thomas: I don't think I should be here today. I don't think this inquisition should be going on. I don't think the FBI files should have been leaked. I don't think that my name should have been destroyed, and I don't think my family and I should have been put through this ordeal, and I don't think our country should be brought low by this garbage. (Committee 4:206–207)

Thomas's alleged sexual behavior in the workplace called into question his capacity for fairness. Perverts cannot be rational deliberators, but, this was Thomas's fifth confirmation hearing for public office. The possibilities revealed by Hill's allegations made suspect the rationality of the appointment process. As Spector said, "The integrity of the Court is very important. It is very important that the Supreme Court not have any member who is tainted or have a cloud. In our society we can accept unfavorable decisions from the Court if we think they are fairly arrived at" (Committee 4:58). To resolve these threats, the senators constructed the "cloud" as an external creation, an alien, malevolent source of defamation and potential systemic infection. The committee needed to forcibly dispel it.

This hearing demonstrated a psychological process of projection. In a remarkable reversal, Hill was transformed from a possible victim of sexual harassment into a coy, fickle, and inconsistent temptress. She became a whimsical seductress who wanted to talk dirty. The committee members repeatedly asked Hill why she did not provide the

FBI or later the committee staff with the detailed (sexual) material that she reported to the committee. Spector's comment was typical of this theme:

> But I also see that your own statement that you prepared in your own leisure, put aside the FBI statement, you were with two people, but no mention of the Coke bottle, no mention about sexual prowess, no mention about other major issues which are in your statement. So I conclude, from looking at this very complex day on our obligation to try to find out what happened between a man and a woman long ago, and nobody else was there, that I would agree with you, Professor Hill, it is very difficult for me to understand. (Committee 4:135)

The committee discounted Hill's explanation that she found discussion of such matters deeply embarrassing (Committee 4:61, 134). This exchange between Spector and Hill was typical:

Ms. Hill: I agree that all of this was not disclosed in the FBI investigation.

Senator Spector: Was it easier for you because one of the FBI agents was a woman, or did you ask at any time that you give the statements to her alone in the absence of the man FBI agent?

Ms. Hill: No, I did not do that. I didn't ask to disclose. I just—I did not.

Senator Spector: Well, I understand from what you are saying now that you were told that you didn't have to say anything if it was too embarrassing for you. My question to you is, did you use that at any point to decline to give any information on the ground that it was too embarrassing?

Ms. Hill: I never declined to answer a question because it was too embarrassing, no. He asked me to describe the incidents, and rather than decline to make any statement at all, I described them to my level of comfort. (Committee 4:62)

Hill's reluctance to disclose fully what she claimed Thomas had said became evidence that she made it up. If Thomas truly had used sexually charged language and behaviors, Hill could have simply and factually reported them, implied Spector. If the language and behavior had been Thomas's, why would Hill have been embarrassed to recount them to the disinterested and objective FBI? For Hill's comfort the FBI even provided a female agent who assured her that the male agent would leave the room "if the questions are too embarrassing" (Committee 4:124).

The absence of detail in Hill's FBI testimony undermined her credibility. For example, Simpson insisted on entering into the record evidence of Hill's "inconsistencies":

> Well, I think that they should know that the witness did not say anything to the FBI about the described size of his penis, the description of the movie *Long Dong Silver*, about the pubic hair in the Coke story, and describing giving pleasures to women with oral sex. That is not part of the original FBI report. And the agents are simply saying that there was no pressure upon the witness, and they specifically say— the woman FBI agent particularly said that she was quite clear that she did not care whether it was general or specific. (Committee 4:124)

Simpson said that such evidence was appropriate "only from the standpoint that you describe in your statement so poignantly that these were disgusting things, and yet they did not appear in the FBI report" (Committee 4:124).

The senators' implication was that Hill was embarrassed because her testimony revealed her, not Thomas's, imagination. Her own fantasy was the source of shame, they implied. It did not reflect a sense of violation or humiliation arising from being a sexualized object. Her reluctance was not an attempt to maintain modesty and civility or to reestablish proper boundaries. She was treated as a tease by the committee, which became the embodiment of the masculine stereotype: it must coax the (falsely) reluctant woman into doing what she wants anyway. By extension, the committee needed to "elicit" the sexually explicit language that Hill longed to use (Committee 4:134).

The rhythm of the testimony resembles a striptease: Hill (not Thomas or the senators) was the generator of sexual material. She wanted to bare all, but gender conventions required that the male senators appear to seduce her. Like other women, however, Hill lacked discipline and self-control; she inevitably went too far. She was eager to use her sexual powers to violate boundaries. What she really wanted was to pollute the public with *her* sexual material. The senators were eager to avow their sexual innocence and the strangeness of her material to them. Hill became the dangerous, sexy woman leading innocent men astray. She tempted them into perverse and degraded territory they would never have entered without her irresistable encouragement. The committee constructed the entire viewing nation as a victim of Hill's sexual harassment.

The tone of the committee's questioning was a remarkable mixture of prurience and disavowal. The absence of detailed language in Hill's statement to the FBI provided an excuse for committee members to repeat certain sexually charged phrases. They blamed Hill for forcing them to talk in such an uncharacteristic manner. The committee members, like Thomas and the witnesses for him, consistently represented themselves as innocents, shocked by the language Hill introduced. Senator Biden did admit "that every woman in America knows that there are men who do say things exactly like what Judge Thomas is accused of saying" (Committee 4:365); however, Thomas's witnesses repeatedly asserted that although this might be so, Thomas had never used such language. He was constitutionally unable to do so, they said (Committee 4:430). Senator Leahy mentioned an article in *The New York Times* concerning Thomas's interest in pornographic movies while he was at Yale Law School. But Thomas's witnesses vehemently agree with former Dean Charles Kothe's statement, "I can't just believe that this man would even think in terms of pornographic movies" (Committee 4:578). Simpson dismissed the significance of *The New York Times* report. He entered into the record a statement by a classmate of Thomas's. Coleman stated "very few" students at Yale Law School failed to attend such films and that "neither she nor the other students were offended by his amusing comments about pornographic material" (Committee 4:584). The obvious contradiction between this statement and that of Kothe, Fitch, and other Thomas witnesses was never explored.

The senators went to great lengths to dissociate themselves from sexual material. Simpson, from Wyoming, stated that students did not attend pornographic films in Laramie, so the material discussed was outside of his experience (Committee 4:584). He found what Hill introduced to be ugly and repugnant, he said (Committee 4:128). Biden said that the content of Hill's charges was difficult to repeat aloud: he had her list them (Committee 4:57–58). He found it "difficult to use" phrases related to sexual behavior (Committee 4:282). Spector said that some of her charges were not too bad, that he could read certain parts (Committee 4:61). He asked her which parts of Thomas's alleged conversations were most embarassing and what she thought was prurient (Committee 4:64). Grassley said that he was relieved that others were questioning Hill about her charges because it was not in his nature to ask such questions (Committee 4:129). Hatch found it embarrassing to use such language in public (Committee 4:162). He claimed that the language was sick and apologizes in advance for repeating it (Committee 4:204). Brown claimed he had not been unmarried for a long enough time to be an expert on contemporary sexual mores (Committee 4:583). Simpson summarized and exemplified this disavowal when he characterized Hill's charges as a "foul, foul stack of stench" (Committee 4:302). Hill was left responsible for the smell.

INSECURE FOUNDATIONS: THE FURIES RETURN

The fact that these allegations concerned two African Americans suggests the pervasiveness of race/gender conflict. Even formerly subordinated men may oppress or injure their supposedly "natural" racial allies. Past discrimination does not always generate a higher level of moral integrity or sensitivity to residual inequalities. Hill's race/gender complicated the committee's response to her allegations. It was difficult for the committee to reconcile race and gender because implicitly the normative woman is white. Because Thomas is African American, race less obviously (from a white position) confounded the interaction between Thomas and Hill. Because they both are black, their conflict appeared to be more straightforward—simply a question of what "happened between a man and a woman" (Committee 4:135). Their shared race, however, put Hill in the position of Woman. Traditionally, white/males extend protection only to some white women (including especially white women who are perceived to be threatened by black men); masculine gender identity as protector is interwoven with racial loyalties and intragender power struggles. Hill could not fit the position historically open to some white women as needing or deserving masculine protection. Thomas could occupy the position of neither male nor black. As male, he could suggest troubling questions about ordinary race/gender behavior. As black, Thomas would revert to a representative of the split off black/male, potentially out of control and a constant threat to white/females. Race loyalty required the senators' attention to sexual harassment, but gender bonding required them to exclude it.

To rescue its legitimacy, the committee permitted Thomas to occupy the position of victim of race/gender injustice while it ratified his claims on triumphant individualism. It acknowledged past struggles between black and white men while it defined men as actual or potential victims of irrational women. The structure and content of the second hearing reflected this mythic construction: the female furies threatening to return and undo (male) political order. The furies are always extrinsic—vengeful, irrational, unpredictable forces, attempting to sink their claws into men. Men tacitly rally against the objects of their desire, and sexuality is located elsewhere (outside of political and economic activity). Sexual harassment charges are now available to women and actionable through law, suggesting a renewed opportunity for women to undermine the social order through misuse of their power. Heterosexual male desire became a potential cause of vulnerability. Simpson discussed the "terrible pain" of thinking of his sons, "rather expansive, stalwart boys"— and the harm women's misuse of power could inflict on his sons (Committee 4:127). More than ever, the senators implied, the security of the public world depended on rational control over female hysteria and sexuality. Men are vulnerable, they suggested, and the problem is not the sexualization of power, domination, and exclusion at the heart of the race/gender contract. It is alien forces that threaten the contract's integrity.

The senators' fierce attacks on Hill reflected primitive fear and panic. Hatch, Spector, Thomas, Doggett, and Biden represented different modes of patriarchy and masculine identity. Hatch represented innocence; Spector was the brave resister/namer/slayer of furies;

Thomas was the wounded victim of feminine irrationality, Doggett was the male who knew women through his superior masculine intuition; and Biden represented paternalism. Hill was both archetypical woman and female/Africanist presence. She embodied all of the negative qualities and dangers attributed to femininity and the specific awful ones of her particular race/gender position. Her fate repeated an ancient pattern in a different way. In expelling Hill and all that she represents, the committee could restore decency and civility (Committee 4:264).

CHAPTER FIVE

The Horror of Blackness: Sleaze, Dirt, and Female Traitors

At the end of the first hearing, Thomas had every reason to believe that he had finally accomplished his goal of "stripping down." He then anticipated full membership in the world of abstract individuals. As he said at the end of that hearing,

> I have been honored to participate in this process. It has been one of the high points—indeed it is the high point from a lifetime of work, a lifetime of effort on behalf of so many people. This is the high point. Whatever your determination is, I would like to reiterate that I have been treated fairly, that I have been honored, deeply honored to participate here. . . . Only in America could this have been possible. Thank you all so much for your courtesy. (Committee 1:521)

In the second hearing, Thomas reminded Biden, "Senator, you stipulated to my character earlier." Biden replied, "I did, and I have again." (Committee 4:223). The first hearing cleansed Thomas of the marks of race/gender. Because of it, he expected unconditional access to the club of abstract individuals. Thomas expected that he would take his place on the highest court of the land, the ultimate locus of rational deliberation. Symbolically cut off at the neck by his black robe, like his fellow justices, he could be a disembodied head.

Like all subordinates, however, Thomas's inauguration into abstract individualism was provisional. The pervasive subtext of white masculinity made his hold on it precarious. Induction of particular subjects into powerful positions does not alter structural power relations; marked subjects retain a liminal status.

One reminder of this status was the patronizing tone occasionally adopted by Hatch and Danforth—two of Thomas's most fervent supporters. In their opening statements, both senators referred to Thomas's body. Unconsciously they could not escape its associations. Hatch remarked that despite Thomas's barefoot childhood, soon he would be able "to put his feet under the bench in the highest court of the land" (Committee 1:43). This statement evoked countless racist jokes centered on black people's feet and their supposed dislike of or discomfort in shoes. Danforth made odd remarks about Thomas's laugh. He said that this laugh was one of the distinctive attributes qualifying Thomas to be a Supreme Court justice. These remarks also roused stereotypical images of black people as minstrels and jokesters:

> I concede that there is something weird about Clarence Thomas. It is his laugh. It is the loudest laugh I have ever heard. It comes from deep inside and it shakes his body, and here is something at least as weird in this most uptight of cities, the object of his laughter is most often himself. (Committee 1:96)

To be initiated into the ruling group, subordinates must exercise continuous self-discipline. They must always consider how dominant subjects may view them. Without such self-regulation, Thomas and others risk expulsion. They can easily revert to their default, subordinate, position. Aspiring and provisional abstract individuals can never feel completely secure. They must be proactive and never neglect their white/male audience. They must continually disprove or elude the dominant construction of black masculinity, including its attributes of irrationality and uncontrollable hypersexuality:

> Well, the difficulty also was that, from my standpoint, is that in this country when it comes to sexual conduct we still have underlying racial attitudes about black men and their views of sex. And once you pin that on me, I can't get it off . . . I made it a point at EEOC and at Education not to play into these stereotypes, at all. I made it a point to have people at those agencies, the black men, the black women to conduct themselves in a way that is not consistent with those stereotypes, and I did the same thing myself. (Committee 4:200)

Imagine Thomas's rage and anguish when it appeared that, despite a lifetime of effort, his induction would be reversed. He could not alone undo this reversal to subordinate status. Once again, he needed to prove his merit to the dominant group. "That is why I am so adamant in this committee about what has been done to me" (Committee 4:200). He said that he had "been able with help of others and with the help of God to defy poverty, avoid prison, overcome segregation, bigotry, racism, obtain one of the finest educations available in this country. But I have not been able to overcome this process" (Committee 4:9).

Hill's charges of sexual harassment marked him in the cruelest manner. They branded him as an out of control, crude, sexual animal—a black/male. Instead of being cleansed, he was covered with mud, spewed with "this nonsense, this garbage, this trash that you siphoned out of the sewers against me" (Committee 4:166). Such evocative language recurred throughout his testimony (see Committee 4:157, 184, 185, 207). Thomas was threatened with being cast into blackness—returning to a subordinate status and suffering its terrible consequences:

> This whole affair has been anguish for me. I feel as though I have been abused in this process, as I said last night, and I continue to feel that way. I feel as though something has been lodged against me and painted on me and it will leave an indelible mark on me. This is something that not only supports but plays into the worst stereotypes about black men in this society. And I have no way of changing it, and no way of refuting these charges. (Committee 4:203)

Thomas's entire strategy in the first hearing—the character defense—threatened to undermine him. Hill's charges called into question his virtuous self-construction. The unauthorized publication of the FBI report "leaked on me, and it is drowning my life, my career, my integrity" (Committee 4:160). Of course he felt that his life had been taken from him: "no horror in my life has been so debilitating" (Committee 4:10). He was right to equate his integrity and his life. His integrity was the basis of his exemption from the prison of race/gender. Thomas could not shake off Hill's accusations because they painted him with the indelible mark of black masculinity. Once returned to that position, he would be powerless to control its consequences. The qualities stereotypically attributed to black/males would make it impossible for him to be a disembodied, rational, abstract individual. To regain his life as an abstract individual, his integrity needed to be reestablished, which was how he justified his anger. His emotional outbursts did not invalidate his earlier character construction. As he said, "There is a difference between approaching a case objectively and watching yourself being lynched. There is no comparison whatsoever" (Committee 4:160). Aggression in the service of virtue was not a vice; it was further evidence of the depth of his virtue. Thomas's anger reflected his moral goodness.

Thomas's attempts to place himself outside of stereotypical black masculinity also made his use of the lynching analogy comprehensible. The regulation of sexuality is a prerequisite for and of power. It is a primary territory on which men contest masculinity and exercise dominance. Such battles between men establish intra- and intergender hierarchies. Thomas said,

In the 1970s I became very interested in the issue of lynching. And if you want to track through this country, in the 19th and 20th centuries, the lynchings of black men, you will see that there is invariably or in many instances a relationship with sex—an accusation that that person cannot shake off. That is the point that I am trying to make. And that is the point that I was making last night that this is high-tech lynching. I cannot shake off these accusations because they play to the worst stereotypes we have about black men in this country. (Committee 4:202)

Even before Hill testified and before Thomas received briefings on the most graphic particulars of her charges, he used lynching analogies. The committee asked Thomas whether he preferred to speak before or after Hill's testimony. Initially, Thomas chose to speak first; however, early in his testimony a dispute arose among committee members. They disagreed about the propriety of quoting the FBI's report of Hill's charges. In compromise, Thomas stepped down and Hill testified. In this brief first appearance, Thomas asserted, "I will not provide rope for my own lynching" (Committee 4:10).

Thomas felt like a lynched person because he, too, faced death. His death would have been a civic, not a physical, one. He frequently reiterated the theme of death: "The last $2\frac{1}{2}$ weeks have been a living hell. I think I have died a thousand deaths" (Committee 4:251). He claimed that he expected attempts on his life after the nomination (Committee 4:249), but then he was truly dead: "The day I get to receive a phone call on Saturday night, last Saturday night, about 7:30 and told that this was going to be in the press, I died. The person you knew, whether you voted for me or against me, died" (Committee 4:251).

Hill's testimony also threatened Thomas with an injury frequently associated with lynching—castration. Her testimony threatened him metaphorically with castration, meaning emasculation and exile from the full powers of dominant subjects. Determining the boundaries of the public domain and controlling the "private parts" of life are important aspects of dominance. The senators and Thomas clearly shared this understanding. Thomas reiterated the association of privacy and phallic power. He would not put his private life on display for "This is not what America is all about." Going beyond questions about his workplace behavior with Hill would violate "fundamental fairness," he said (Committee 4:9). Early in the second hearing, Biden reassured Thomas, that he "will not be asked to" discuss any matters Thomas considered private (Committee 4:27). When Leahy asked whether Thomas ever discussed pornography with any other woman, Thomas exploded, "Senator, I will not get into any discussions that I might have about my personal life or my sex life with any person outside of the workplace" (Committee 4:195). Leahy reassured him that this was not what he was asking; he insisted that Thomas's "personal life" was his (Committee 4:195).

The senators understood that privacy means respecting territory. Respect for Thomas included not forcing his public association with sexuality. Only inferior others are so marked. Thomas correctly associated sexual harassment charges with humiliation, which stems not only from harassment's connotations of public sexuality but also from patriarchal duties of protection and representation. As a father, he represented the whole family. Insult to him injured his entire family:

"My family has been humiliated enough. I have been humiliated enough" (Committee 4:241). Heflin responded sympathetically, "All right, I will respect you. Whatever you want to state and however you want to answer it" (Committee 4:241).

These associations of privacy with power shaped Thomas's combative stance in his first statement. He attempted to recover status by immediately claiming control over the sexual terrain:

> I will not provide the rope for my own lynching or for further humiliation. I am not going to to engage in discussions, nor will I submit to roving questions of what goes on in the most intimate parts of my private life or the sanctify of my bedroom. These are the most intimate parts of my privacy, and will remain just that, private (Committee 4:10).

Although he might not have escaped this high-tech lynching, Thomas would allow no one to attack *his* private parts. Even while confronting a thousand deaths, Thomas would

> rather die than withdraw from this process. Not for the purpose of serving on the Supreme Court but for the purpose of not being driven out of this process. I will not be scared. I don't like bullies. I have never run from bullies. I never cry uncle and I am not going to cry uncle today whether I want to be on the Supreme Court or not (Committee 4:252).

Interestingly, the committee members respectfully accepted this stirring avowal of masculine prowess together with Thomas's claim that he was a victim. In his opening statement during the second hearing, Thomas said,

> Mr. Chairman, I am a victim of this process and my name has been harmed, my integrity has been harmed, my character has been harmed, my family has been harmed, my friends have been harmed. There is nothing this committee, this body or this country can do to give me my good name back, nothing (Committee 4:9).

Within the previously agreed-upon narrative, he had indeed been demoted. He had been admitted into the brotherhood through what he persistently called his "real" hearing (the first one). He angrily admonished the committee, "Think about who you are talking to" (Committee 4:263). Then, simply on the word of a woman, white/ males were persecuting him. To restore his integrity and his status as an abstract individual, he needed to regain race/gender privilege. One power of full masculinity is to separate from the irrationally driven body. Another is to escape sexual vulnerability by controlling women's potential manipulation of it. Males do not allow females to affect their standing in the intragender hierarchy. Therefore, women—not men—are marked as sexual beings.

Although Thomas rejected the dominant account of black/male sexuality, he made full use of stereotypes about women. Women are "the sex," and, as such, they cannot represent the whole. Marked as "the sex," black/females (and Hill in particular) cannot represent "the race." With the universalizing magic of masculinity, only black/males can represent the race. These assumptions shape one of Thomas's central speeches. He declared,

> There was an FBI investigation. This is not an opportunity to talk about difficult matters privately or in a closed environment. This is a circus. It is a national disgrace. And from my standpoint, as a black American, as far as I am concerned, it is a high-tech lynching for uppity blacks who in any way deign to think for themselves, to do for themselves, to have different ideas, and that unless you kow-tow to an older order, this is what will happen to you, you will be lynched, destroyed, caricatured by a committee of the U.S. Senate, rather than hung from a tree (Committee 4:157–158).

This statement was remarkable for several reasons. Most of the ways in which Thomas characterized himself also applied to Hill. She was a conservative Republican and defended Robert Bork. She served in a Republican administration. She could have kow-towed to an older order by remaining silent and not disturbing existing race/gender relations. By testifying before the committee, Hill exposed herself to caricature and public humiliation. Here, however, Thomas positioned himself as *the* black American. In the first hearing, he had insisted he had never benefited from his race/gender. Later, when it supported his claim to victimization, Thomas appropriated subordination's full moral weight. In Thomas's account, the lynched black/male exemplified America's racial history. He erased the experiences of other subjects in this story, including the sexual violence suffered by black/females. The actual lynching of black subjects, male and female, were trivialized.

The fact that Thomas's ultimate accuser is a black woman, not a committee composed of fourteen white/males, produced certain discontinuities. Neither Thomas nor the senators acknowledged the race/gender specifics of lynching. The sexual accusations against black/males to which Thomas alluded were made by or for white/females. Whites, mostly white/males, lynched black/males. No men, black or white, were ever lynched on the word of or to defend a black/female.

These contradictions were handled by either erasing Hill's race/gender or impugning her for race/gender disloyalty. Sometimes in relation to Thomas, the black subject, she became a generic woman. By positioning himself as the only subordinate, Thomas set Hill up as a victimizer, someone who could therefore never be a victim. When Kohl pointed out that Hill is an African American, Thomas did not respond directly. He continued to complain that he was being wronged (Committee 4:263). Thomas so thoroughly represented the universal, he became the "wronged" subject, drawing on common connotations of the wronged woman.

Despite his newly claimed, honored race/gender status, Thomas was willing to sacrifice a black woman. This sacrifice was not a moral lapse. According to dominant race/gender arrangements, Hill deserved neither his protection nor his loyalty. As a black/woman, Hill failed twice. She did not stand behind her man, therefore violating basic rules. Black/females have the additional charge of "upholding" the race. Failure to stand behind their men, the representatives of the race, undermines the well-being of the whole group. Losing the backing of "their" women creates even greater disadvantage for black/males. Weakening its representative undermines the race. Thomas said that he would mourn her "betrayal," but he expressed no reciprocal obligation of loyalty. Only *she* was the race traitor.

Thomas claimed moral weight for himself, but his approach was contradictory. By obscuring the historical particulars, he shifted blame away from the actual committee members to the more abstract "committee"; to the "process", or, preferably, to Hill. This shift preserved a tactful space in which he could renegotiate solidarity with his white/male interrogators. The committee became a fraternal group, not a lynch mob. Many supporters and defenders of Thomas's ideas were white/males. Danforth, who committee members called a "tower of integrity" (Committee 4:265), was one of his mentors and, of course, George Bush nominated him. Moreover, some of his strongest critics were black leaders.

This strategy made sense in the context of existing power relations. Only white/males could readmit Thomas into the charmed circle of abstract individuals, so it was not in Thomas's interest to antagonize them. To maintain alliance with the senators while using his race/gender status to his own benefit, he portrayed them as fellow victims. They were all casualties of "this process," he said. He and the senators were victims of leaks to the media, of an apparently calculated public disclosure of material meant to remain secret.

They were also all potential victims of women, Thomas implied. Because sexual harassment had become an injury remedied by law, white/males, not just black ones, were vulnerable to women's irrational or vengeful behavior. These laws against sexual harassment potentially altered the traditional race/gender balance of power. The female tendency to play unfairly threatens all males. Women can lodge false charges against white/males as easily as black ones. If Hill were willing to betray one of her own race, would white women not engage in similar behavior? This possibility provided a new basis for race/gender solidarity. The second hearing has shown Thomas "just how vulnerable I am as a human being, and any American, that these kind of charges can be given validation in a process such as this, and the destruction it can do" (Committee 4:256).

Thomas's outrage that the committee had not considered these "difficult matters" in private represented an appeal to the senators as fellow victims. They shared with him an interest in controlling women like Hill. The committee should not have allowed Hill to define the issues. Her allegations were not an appropriate topic of public discussion. The committee had already agreed to define sexual harassment as a "personal" relationship between men and women. It does not structure or concern the public domain. Hill's charges should have been treated as "family" matters in a "private" space (among men).

Equating fairness of the system with fairness to Thomas put forth a subtle threat. He could expose the dream as an illusion. The second hearing was inflicting a far bigger hurt on the United States than on himself, he suggested. It called into question the goodness of the entire system (Committee 4:251–252). The hearing was undermining his belief in the country and its fairness (Committee 4:251). In the first hearing, Thomas had "faith that, at least this system was working in some fashion, though imperfectly" (Committee 4:251). If a black/male, already confirmed four times by the Senate, could not receive his just rewards, who could? He issued a challenge to the senators to prove that the American dream was not false. Having set himself up as proof, rejecting him would have disproved the dream. Because the senators had agreed to the first proposition, they had to accept its logical consequence.

The committee responded in kind. It profferred courtesies to Thomas never extended by lynch mobs. The senators rushed to reassure him, that his faith was not misguided. Simpson, for example, said, "There is truth out there and it is in the judicial system. Thank God that there is such a system. It has saved many, many a disillusioned person who was, you know, headed for the Stygian pits" (Committee 4:254). If Hill had been required to go through a "real" judicial process, they suggested she would have been destroyed (Committee 4:254). Although the committee had reconvened to listen to Hill's accusations and Thomas's responses the senators reassured Thomas that he was presumed innocent. In the first hearing, Heflin discussed "doubting Thomas"; in this situation, as Simpson said, "If there is any doubt, it goes to Clarence Thomas. It does not go to Professor Hill" (Committee 4:189). Biden even tried to establish the hearing as common ground. He stated that the committee was simply doing what Thomas himself would do at the EEOC. Just because the senators felt they had to investigate the charges did not mean that they believed them. Biden appealed to Thomas as a fellow professional: it "would have been irresponsible" when faced with someone of "Professor Hill's standing and background" not to investigate (Committee 4:187).

The senators courtesy also furthered their interests. Thomas's rebukes of a "high-tech lynching" reminded the senators of their privileged positions. White/males can block black ones from the brotherhood. They can punish black/males for ordinary male behavior or deny them customary male defenses. Black/males accurately interpret this white/male privilege as an unfair exclusion. By vindicating Thomas, the senators rescued themselves and the nation from charges of exclusion. They redeemed "the process" and the American dream.

CHAPTER SIX

"At Least McCarthy Was Elected": Fraternal Reconciliation

Thomas had established the tone for the rest of the hearing. Although Kennedy and Metzenbaum made critical comments, they were in the minority. DiConcini denounced the "atrocious process" they had all experienced. Hatch claimed that Thomas was a victim of a double standard and that the attacks on him were not decent (Committee 4:250). The senators portrayed Thomas as the unjustly accused and the harassed victim, and Hatch asked Thomas how this reversal felt. Simpson also saw a reversal and said that Thomas was wise not to listen to Hill's charges, for "There is not a woman alive who would take the questions you have had to take, would be just repelled by it" (Committee 4:254). The hearings were a disgusting tragedy, the senators stated. Simpson likened Thomas to Othello and quoted from Shakespeare about the pain at having one's good name stolen. This analogy is revealing, for Desdemona, Othello's wife and the object of his fatal jealousy, is a white woman. Shakespeare's Othello realizes too late that his real enemy is Iago, not his wife. This analogy implicitly accepted Thomas's displacement of Hill. It reinforced Thomas's exclusive possession of the race/gender victim role, and it also resonated with another public matter that Thomas and the senators kept private: Thomas's second wife is a white woman. Biden introduced her to the committee, and she attended the hearings; but almost never did anyone mention her race.

We were on a reestablished, shared masculine/individual terrain. The senators readmitted Thomas by defining him as a peer—a fellow lawyer, an expert on sexual harassment and women, a patriarch, and an American hero. The senators and Thomas bonded in battle against their true harasser—Anita Hill.

Thomas actively asserted a series of contradictory positions, all affirmed by the senators. He successfully defined himself as an expert both on the crime of which he was accused and on the woman who accused him. He positioned himself as a victim not of white men but of a (black) woman. He presented himself as a nurturing father who was betrayed by a child/employee. He described himself as maintaining cordial relations with Hill, even though she was vindictive, out to get him, and angry. Race was never the cause of his nomination, he said, yet he may have been undone by a racist plot. He enjoyed an equal and intimate relationship with the senators, yet he was being lynched by their process. He was an insider and confirmed for a series of powerful positions, yet he was an outsider, vulnerable to abuse. Thomas claimed to be punished for being uppity and independent and still being just like his listeners. He was a martyr and a survivor. Thomas was a former EEOC chairman, an expert on and also one with zero tolerance for sexual harassment; however, he was furious that the committee was even investigating Hill's charges (Committee 4:263).

Progressively distancing himself from Hill, Thomas established his proximity to the senators. Like them, he was a sensitive champion of women. He frequently used a familial, paternal language and described himself as his family's protector. He shared the senators' belief that women are territory about which men are experts. He and the senators were fellow lawyers preparing for a case and trying to ascertain the motives of a hostile witness.

Thomas also appealed to a shared masculine vulnerability. A woman could destroy any man in the room. Because Hill was placed symbolically as the generic woman, all men could imagine being undone by her. The plight of an uppity black was transmuted into a condition that anyone with visible power could experience. Power exposes all men to this potentially dangerous, negative side of independence. "If it can happen to me, it can happen to anybody, any time, over any issue" (Committee 4:185).

The senators were eager to agree with Thomas's presentation. They present themselves as family men, dedicated to his values of decency and fairness. Only duty could remove them from their decency and force them to repeat the awful language Hill alleged. They were equals with Thomas all sexually innocent and suffering through the process with him. They were objective experts on material foreign to their own experience. While describing themselves as zealous and sensitive defenders of women, the senators and Thomas did not hesitate to use many traditional denigrations of women. While discussing extensively and denouncing stereotypes of black male sexuality, they constructed Hill as the instigator of race/gender subordination (Committee 4:201–207). She, not white men, threatened to lynch an "uppity black." The senators bonded to rescue a brother.

From "No More Excuses" to Vulnerability/Victim

Thomas's tone shifted after Hill's testimony. Initially, he had been somewhat conciliatory. He had said that if "there is anything that I have said that has been misconstrued by Anita Hill or anyone else to be sexual harassment, then I can say I am so very sorry" (Committee 4:8). Thomas had wished he had known that his behavior was being interpreted incorrectly. If he had known, he would have stopped immediately. He had implied that he could exercise good judgment, empathy, and self-control. The error was in Hill's interpretation of his behavior.

When Thomas returned to the hearing room to testify after Hill, his rage was evident. Despite his prior claim that participating in the first hearing had been an honor, he said that the entire process had been an ordeal he "endured . . . for 103 days" (Committee 4:8). More than 100 days after the nomination, its honor was crushed. The price had been too high, and he had suffered immensely from the charges against him. He described this suffering in Promethean terms: "I have been wracking my brains, and eating my insides out trying to think of what I could have said or done to Anita Hill to lead her to allege that I was interested in her in more than a professional way, and that I talked to her about pornographic films" (Committee 4:6). Only God was powerful enough to help Thomas through this time, he said, and "God is my judge, not you, Senator Metzenbaum" (Committee 4:237). Thomas emphatically denied every allegation that suggested that he had had sexual conversations or discussed pornography. He had not pressured Hill to date him and had had no personal interest in her.

In Thomas's opening statement, he said that when he had heard the charges and who had made them, he had been shocked, surprised, hurt, and saddened. Since that day, he had not been the same. Thomas called on the strength that helped get him from Pin Point, Georgia, to the Senate hearing room. Even his strength was waning, he said (Committee 4:5). The nomination process had destroyed what took him forty-three years to build. The pain he felt, stemmed from two sources—a friend's disloyalty and his dedication to protecting women's rights. Betrayal by anyone other than a friend might have made his plight easier, he said. He had spent almost a decade enforcing the rights of sexual harassment victims. After feeling so strongly and speaking so loudly about the issue at the EEOC, enduring such charges was doubly hard. He had not been able to listen to Hill's testimony, although he had a summary of it and his wife had watched significant portions (Committee 4:191). Even some of Thomas's supporters were surprised that he had not listened to the testimony of his accuser, but Thomas replied that he had not been able to take anymore: "There is only so much a human being can take. . . . I wish there was more for me to give, but I have given all I can" (Committee 4:234). The subtext Thomas initiated at this point was further developed later, throughout the hearing. He had been so good that any charges against him were evidence of persecution. He had always complied with the rules. He had cooperated fully with the committee, and his behavior had been exemplary. As a "boss, as a friend, as a human being" he was proud that he had "never had such an allegation leveled against" him (Committee 4:5).

Thomas said that the day was "a travesty" (Committee 4:157). He suggested that an interest group invented the story and was leading the plot (Committee 4:252). He had claimed, "I do not share your view that this was not concocted" (Committee 4:237). Furthermore, Thomas said that Hill's "story was developed to harm me . . . and it did harm me" (Committee 4:253). He complained that the hearing was not in a closed room, but he assured the committee, "I can heal . . . I will survive. My question was, will the country survive, and hopefully it will" (Committee 4:256). He should not have to defend himself, he argued, he should not even be in the room. The guilty were elsewhere, and the harm lay in even entertaining Hill's charges.

The committee staff, not Thomas, should be the defendants, he said. The staffers should be brought in "to confront the people in this country for this kind of effort, and I think that they should at some point have to confront my family" (Committee 4:230). "This has caused me great pain and my family great pain" (Committee 4:257).

Thomas was concerned not for African Americans or for himself but for the integrity of the nation and its political processes. He shared his concern: "You should feel worse for the country than you do for me" (Committee 4:185). Hatch replied, "I feel bad for both" (Committee 4:185). Whereas Thomas was a victim of the process, he said, his suffering could lead to improvements for the country (Committee 4:249).

Thomas frequently articulated his concern for the country:

> I think the country has been hurt by this process. I think we are destroying our institutions. And I think it is a sad day when the U. S. Senate can be used by hate mongers and people who are interested in digging up dirt to destroy other people and who will stop at no tactics, when they use our great political institutions for their political ends, we have gone far beyond McCarthyism. This is far more dangerous than McCarthyism. At least McCarthy was elected. (Committee 4:184; see also Committee 4:251)

Thomas's not-very-subtle message was that race/gender loyalty should be reconstructed and that the political system could not endure overt, public displays of its internal civil war. The Senate, and by extension other political institutions, could not allow people not even in the club to destroy them. This hearing was worse than the greatest dangers of McCarthyism because "at least McCarthy was elected" (Committee 4:184). McCarthy was, however, a problem—he was one of their own.

Most of the senators accepted Thomas's representations and even shared his view of them as victims. When power is threatened, even the powerful adopt the language of victimization. Leahy said that he was "not happy with the process"; similarly, it affected Danforth, a "tower of integrity," and others (Committee 4:265). Danforth empathized with Thomas and his family, namely his son and wife. "As a

U. S. senator—I do not like at all the way we have been brought here" (Committee 4:265). DeConcini said, "I can't believe I am here myself. I can't believe that this process is taking place . . . I am ashamed to be part of this process" (Committee 4:256). The process was pointless, they claimed, because awareness of sexual harassment already existed. Kohl called the hearings "a collective travail" (Committee 4:262), and Biden bids his members to stop complaining. Democracy is lousy, he said, "except that nobody has figured out another way" (Committee 4:266). Nonetheless he admonished them within the shared discourse of masculine power: "We are big boys" (Committee 4:267). When he ran for President, he knew he would be fair game. Anyone appointed to the court should understand "this is not Boy Scouts. It is not Cub Scouts," he reminded the committee (Committee 4:267).

Thomas was a fellow lawyer and an expert, possessing knowledge that the committee needed to conduct its investigation. Biden apologized for the process, but said that as a fellow expert Thomas could understand that in some cases there was often no corroborating evidence (Committee 4:268). Like Thomas, the Senate must do its job even in difficult cases. The law requires judgment (Committee 4:237).

"This Is Not Boy Scouts, It Is Not Cub Scouts"

The committee engaged Thomas in extensive speculation about Hill's motives. The members and Thomas conversed like law partners developing a strategy for a difficult trial. Spector, for example, enlisted Thomas to help prepare a charge of perjury against Hill (Committee 4:232–239). He asked Thomas to identify which statements in Hill's testimony were not credible or consistent. Could the conflicts in their testimony simply be a matter of seeing the same behavior differently, he asked. Thomas rejected this suggestion, saying that it was not a matter of perspectives as none of the behaviors Hill alleged occurred (Committee 4:239).

The emphasis was on Hill's credibility. The committee asked Thomas few questions about the particulars of her charges, and they pointed out none of the inconsistencies between Thomas's testimony in the first and later hearings. Their questions are posed apologetically, marked with their respect for Thomas, reluctance to insult him, and distaste for their task. Hatch said that he "hates to go into it," and Thomas shared Hatch's distaste: "I would not want to, except being required to here, to dignify those allegations with a response. As I have said before, I categorically deny them. To me, I have been pilloried with scurrilous allegations of this nature" (Committee 4:161–162). Hatch continued his questioning with reluctance: "This is embarrassing for me to say in public, but it has to be done, and I am sure it is not pleasing to you . . . did you ever say in words or substance something like there is a pubic hair in my Coke?" (Committee 4:161–162).

Hatch and Thomas agreed that such material is outside of normal behavior. Everyone who listened to Hill wanted to like her, Hatch said, and "many do." Although she presented herself well, however, her testimony did not comply with common experience. For Hill's allegations to be true, the accused person would have to "be a psychopathic sex fiend or a pervert," said Hatch (Committee 4:200). Thomas agreed and noted that if he used such language, it would affect other aspects of his life and reputation (Committee 4:201). Hatch implied that as it is obvious Thomas is neither a pervert nor a psychopath, Hill has made up the behaviors she described. Perhaps *she* was the sex fiend.

A substantial number of the senators' questions to Thomas pertain to Hill's motives for lying (see, for example, the exchanges between Thurmond and Thomas [Committee 4:227], Spector and Thomas [Committee 4:228–234], Leahy and Thomas, [Committee 4:242], Grassley and Thomas [Committee 4:258], and Simon and Thomas [Committee 4:259]). Hatch said that Thomas had the right to point out inconsistencies in Hill's testimony, even though she is a "nice person" (Committee 4:161). Heflin said that Thomas could help the committee prove that Hill was lying and asked Thomas about Hill's motives. Thomas participated in these dialogues, stating, for example, that Hill is not a civil rights zealot. Thomas qualified this statement by insisting that the committee had "an obligation to determine why [they] would allow uncorroborated, unsubstantiated allegations to ruin [his] life" (Committee 4:186). He expressed exasperation at the task the committee had invited him to join; he could not prove that something had not occurred.

Thomas, like his questioners, speculated freely about Hill's motives while disavowing his desire to consider them. This seeming contradiction enabled him to make allegations that appealed to the senators without being held accountable for them. Thomas suggested, for example, that Hill may have been displeased with him for dating and appointing women "with lighter complexions" (Committee 4:264). Or, he suggested, she could have been harboring anger over lost access and importance to Thomas when he moved to the EEOC. Motives such as these provide little basis for such betrayal, he said, and he remained perplexed by her allegations. When Hill worked for Thomas, he said, "she was not perfect, but there seemed to me nothing that would suggest that she would do this to me" (Committee 4:187). This mixture of subtle denigration and patronizing tolerance was typical of Thomas's language about Hill. Heflin asked whether Thomas had any evidence that Hill could lose her grasp on reality, and Thomas replied that one employee at the EEOC had warned him that Hill was his "enemy." He had, however, remained loyal to her: "I refused to believe that and argued with him [the employee] about that and refused to act in accordance with that" (Committee 4:187). Thomas also denied making any inferences concerning Hill as he was not a psychiatrist or a psychologist but a busy agency chair (Committee 4:188).

The senators treated Thomas as a character expert as well. He subtly constructed a picture of a competent but erratic young woman who sometimes lacked self-control and objectivity. She had difficulty maintaining professional distance and had an exaggerated sense of her own abilities, he revealed. Her "work was good . . . it was not as good as some of the other members of the staff" (Committee 4:168). Hill's ambition exceeded her capacities and, because of her inexperience, she was not high in the "pecking order" at the EEOC, he said, adding that this lack of status troubled her (Committee 4:221). In 1983, Hill had sought a promotion to be Thomas's chief of staff. When she was not chosen, she "was concerned about it," said Thomas (Committee 4:168). Thomas also revealed that Hill tended to get upset when she did not get her way. As a staff member, she would take firm positions and, when disagreements arose, as Thomas portrayed it, she behaved childishly. He described Hill as "unyielding to other members of the staff, and then storming off or throwing a temper tantrum of some sort that either [he] or the chief of staff would have to iron out" (Committee 4:168). Hill had trouble engaging in rational argument, said Thomas, who described her as becoming "a bit irate" and "adamant" about their differences concerning quotas (Committee 4:248–249).

Thomas also constructed a picture of Hill as unarousing, unappealing, and lacking femininity. Hatch asked how Hill's colleagues at the EEOC felt about her, and Thomas replied, "somewhat distant and perhaps aloof" (Committee 4:168). Therefore, by inference, Hill was unlikely to evoke a man's erotic interest. She was too distant, tough, and willful to be a victim or a sexual object (even though his own toughness did not protect him from this fate). Heflin characterized Hill as a meek woman, but Thomas corrected him: "That is not as I remember Anita . . . Anita would not have been considered a meek woman. She was an aggressive debater. She stood her ground. When she got her dander up, she would storm off and I would say that she is a bright person, a capable person. Meek is not a characterization that I would remember" (Committee 4:186). He also said that she was "aggressive, strong, and forceful in advocating the positions that she stood for" (Committee 4:186). Furthermore, Hill was too unapproachable to be sexually harassed, although simultaneously, Thomas denied any negative implications about Hill. He refused to "sit here with the committee and attempt to criticize" her character (Committee 4:187). Unlike Hill, Thomas was too good to stoop to character assassination.

Despite Thomas's declaration that his personal life was out of bounds, he and Hatch discussed dating behavior. Hatch described Hill as "an extremely intelligent woman and from all appearances a lovely human being." He asked, "Do you think an intelligent African American male, like you, or any other intelligent male, regardless of race, would use this kind of language to try and start a relationship with an intelligent, attractive woman?" (Committee 4:202). Thomas replied, "Senator, I don't know anyone who would try to establish a relationship with that kind of language." Hatch emphasized his solidarity with Thomas on this point: "I don't even know people who might have emotional disturbances who would try this" (Committee 4:202). If Thomas had been interested in dating Hill, he would not have used such language, and because he had not been interested in dating her, he would not have violated the boundaries of a professional relationship. By definition, professional relationships are not sexual; therefore, whatever his motive, Thomas could not have sexually harassed Hill.

As an expert on sexual harassment, Thomas should have known that sexual harassment, like lynching, is about power. It is not about dating etiquette, sexual desire, or private relationships between men and women. Sexualized behavior is employed for the purposes of domination. Its intent is to control its object, not to make love to it. Nonetheless, Thomas persistently positioned himself as an expert on sexual harassment. He assured (and threatened) his listeners that there was "no member of this committee or this Senate who feels stronger about sexual harassment than [he did]" (Committee 4:163). Thomas stated that he had witnessed sexual harassment. Once he had attained a powerful position, it had been his policy to fire immediately any person who engaged in it (Committee 4:194). He could not possibly have engaged in offenses he had been appointed (and approved by them) to regulate. His expertise enabled him to evaluate his own conduct and he could assist the senators in rendering judgment on him.

Some of the senators invited Thomas's expertise. Hatch said, "I have known you for eleven years, and you are an expert in sexual harassment" (Committee 4:163). Leahy also treated Thomas as an expert, questioning him about the normal pattern of sexual harassment and whether an investigator typically finds such behavior directed toward only one person. Thomas explained that there usually is a pattern, with a series of incidents emerging and extending over time (Committee 4:195). No one accused Thomas of a pattern of harassment. Investigators had not found any evidence to support a series of incidents. Lieberman, who was not a committee member, even ordered a survey of Thomas's female employees, because, as Hatch said, "He has to be as appalled by these accusations as I am, and frankly he wanted to know, 'Just what kind of a guy is Clarence Thomas?' And those of us who know you, know that all of these are inconsistent with the real Clarence Thomas" (Committee 4:165). None of the employees surveyed complained of sexual harassment; therefore, Hill must have made up her allegations, which did not comply with the expert's description of the norm.

Hatch consulted Thomas about whether Hill should have pressed charges and the routes available to her at the Department of Education and the EEOC. They discussed the fairness of statutory limits on such charges, given the limits of memory and the unavailability of firm evidence. Hatch and Thomas agreed that the charges Hill had leveled were so appalling that no one would have tolerated them or continued to work with a person who would commit them (Committee 4:164). This belief was fact to them; however, Thomas also testified that when he had been in less powerful positions, he had observed sexual harassment and had been unable to stop it (Committee 4:194). Thomas also was questioned about Earl Harper, Jr., a senior trial lawyer who was with the EEOC in Baltimore during Thomas's term as chairman. Harper had been accused by "some twelve or thirteen women who claim that (he) made unwelcome sexual advances to several women on his staff, including instances in which Mr. Harper masturbated in the presence of some female employees. The allegations contain other aspects of sexual activity" (Committee 4:158). Following a lengthy investigation, the EEOC general counsel recommended firing Harper. For reasons that remained unclear and contested by Thomas, Harper retained his position for eleven months after this recommendation and then retired. The committee did not pursue the relevance of this or other cases to Thomas's description of sexual harassment. Biden ruled them irrelevant, but he and Thomas discussed extensively the nature of sexual harassment and Thomas's commitment to combatting it with EEOC initiatives and other means. Biden also insisted that neither sexual harassment nor Thomas's tenure as head of the EEOC were relevant. All that mattered were Hill's allegations against Thomas and Thomas's conduct toward her. Evidently, general issues, policies, and related cases were relevant only when they exculpated Thomas.

Some of the senators also treated Thomas as an expert on another form of sexual harassment: the use of race/gender stereotypes against black/males. Ascribed expertise in this area allowed Thomas to play the race card again. He blamed Hill for these stereotypes and accused her of employing the most damaging stereotypes about black/male sexuality. Furthermore, he redefined her situation: she had not been humiliated and demeaned: Thomas had. Hatch methodically reviewed Hill's testimony with Thomas, asking him to identify the stereotypes in each charge. Thomas named discussions of the frequency of sex, sexual prowess, and the size of sexual organs (including references to *Long Dong Silver*) stereotypes. Hatch drew a parallel between these charges and a sexual harassment case from the tenth circuit in which a black woman was "subjected to numerous racial slurs and epithets" by a white/male defendant (Committee 4:204). Hatch and Thomas agreed that in the present situation Thomas was the abused (Committee 4:202).

Moral Worth: Character Defense

Thomas's character defense reappeared in a new guise in this hearing. He was congenitally unable to engage in sexual harassment. Character also provided reason for the committee's obligation to listen to Hill's charges. Biden said, "We have two very credible people with very, very diverse positions on an issue" (Committee 4:215). Hill appears to be a credible witness. She is a tenured professor at a law school; even Thomas viewed her as a credible person before this. If the committee did not provide a forum for her charges, it would be vulnerable to questions about its own credibility. The committee has equated character and credibility.

As Spector reiterated the problem was that the two witnesses had very different stories and no one else observed "this tragedy" (Committee 4:228). The only way to explain the differing accounts was that one of the two must have been lying or fantasizing. When other evidence is lacking, said Spector, the determination of merit rests on individual credibility. The committee had already confirmed Thomas's integrity and could not reverse its judgment solely on the word of one woman. Despite Hill's intelligence and position as a law professor, she was the only person other than Thomas who knew if her charges were true (Committee 4:184). Without overwhelming evidence to support Hill's claims, the presumption of virtue, and therefore innocence, must remain with Thomas. The committee members reminded one another of their previously agreed upon characterization of Thomas's moral excellence. Hatch, for example, stated,

> This has come down to this, one woman's allegations that are ten years old against your lifetime of service over that same ten year period. I have known you almost eleven years. And the person that the good professor described is not the person I have known . . . how this could have happened. How one person's uncorroborated allegations could destroy a career and one of the most wonderful opportunities for a young man from Pin Point, Georgia (Committee 4:184)

Thomas and his supporters portrayed him as deeply moral, superior to even members of Congress in his ethical committments and behavior. His behavior exceeded dominant norms, and he was the antithesis of the hypersexual, irrational, uncontrollable black/male stereotype. Hatch claimed that Thomas had an outstanding record, better than that of Congress, on hiring women (Committee 4:165). Although everyone deplored sexual harassment, Hatch pointed out, unlike many others, Thomas and the EEOC were doing something about it. Thomas had "been a champion in this area for women. [He had] been a champion in many ways for a lot of [them]" (Committee 4:214). A champion of race/gender justice could never have engaged in the oppression he had dedicated himself to fighting, implied Hatch.

Thomas assertively deployed his character defense. He claimed that he was far less concerned about losing an appointment to the Supreme Court than about having his integrity destroyed. Part of the "shock, dismay, hurt, and pain" (Committee 4:184) Hill's charges caused him was because such an act violated one of his own most prized ethical commitments—loyalty. He had thought highly of Hill and had done his best for her. Her betrayal was "an enormously painful experience and it is one when you ask yourself, you rip at yourself, what could you have done? And why could this happen or why would it happen?" (Committee 4:184).

Thomas implied that Hill was unethical and did not even fight fairly. The proceedings were a tragedy, he said, because Hill had chosen to lodge charges against him for which there was no defense (Committee 4:134). Unlike her, he was never vindictive, and he had never threatened to ruin her career (Committee 4:128). Unlike Hill, to him, "loyalty is something that was important" (Committee 4:188). Hill's accusations ought to raise questions about her character, not his, he charged. If Hill betrayed Thomas, who had worked so hard for her, then Hill's character was dubious.

Ethical issues were so important to Thomas that he never "play[ed] games"—one slur and he fired the employee (Committee 4:255). He never discussed pornography in the workplace, nor would he tell a joke that any person would find offensive (Committee 4:196, 222). If he was ever inadvertently insensitive, he would want to be told immediately so he could correct his behavior. Thomas provided an example to illustrate the depth of his commitment to a comfortable environment for his staff. He had not been aware that a short staff member had been unable to reach the elevator buttons. Instead, she had had to walk up the stairs until she had told him that she could not reach the buttons. He cited his grandfather to emphasize his reaction: "It is that kind of insensitivity, oversight, and I made it a point to tell my staffers, if I do something, let me know what it is. If you see something, tell me what it is so that we can correct it. If you hear something, tell me what it is. My grandfather used to have a statement. I can read your letter, but I can't read your mind" (Committee 4:222).

Biden suggested that Thomas would not even engage in the kind of talk that men enjoy when no women are in the room. Women comprised most of Thomas's staff:

I could not tolerate individuals making that environment uncomfortable or hostile. I could not tolerate individuals who had to segregate their language or conduct in order to get along. The conduct had to be purged of offensive attitudes and I made that a constant effort, and that's something that I was proud of and it was something I am sure the people who worked with me felt comfortable with and understood. (Committee 4:223)

Thomas's concern for other's comfort is further evidence of his "special sensitivity." If Hill had ever complained to him or to others about him, then even the most trivial offense would have immediately become the object of his reparation. His own experiences with segregation and racial slurs had made him a better person and heightened his dedication to creating a better environment for others. Even this atrocious hearing will deepen his sensitivity, he said, claiming that the second hearing and its egregious violation of his rights had heightened his awareness of the importance of privacy. Ironically, considering his subsequent Supreme Court decisions, he also said that he would be more protective of the accused's rights (Committee 4:257).

"THEY ARE FAMILY"

The language of family and private matters pervaded the testimony. Although Thomas had declared his private life off limits; he was eager to use aspects of it in his defense. The boundaries between public and private shifted, depending on what benefited him. In this hearing, as elsewhere in politics, family values simultaneously served public purposes and private power arrangements. In the name of privacy and the family, public institutions reinforced patriarchal power.

Three dimensions of paternity were particularly salient. Thomas constructed himself as a normal family man. He was both an outraged family protector and family to Hill. A subset of paternity is power to engage in the traffic in women.[1] Women are objects to be circulated among men. The purpose of this exchange of women is to foster ties among men. Women are simply instruments to cementing these ties. Their exchanges affirm and strengthen bonds of obligation and friendship among men. In this instance, as Thomas saw it, Hill was a gift from Gil Hardy, one of Thomas's closest friends. Harassing Hill would have insulted Hardy, a betrayal a man would never inflict on a brother. Hill "came to me through one of my dearest, dearest friends—he was the best man at my wedding" (Committee 4:197). Thomas's relationship to Hardy created a profound obligation to Hill:

When he brought her to my attention, it was a special responsibility that he asked me to take on, and I felt very strongly that I could discharge that in the way that I did, and that was to be careful about her career, to make sure she had opportunities, to be there to offer advice and counsel, and that is something that I continued with my other special assistants. They are family. (Committee 4:197)

Paternity is central to Thomas. One reason he would survive the hearings, he said, despite the thousand deaths they have inflicted on him, is that he would regain his life. In an interesting race/gender role reversal, he insisted that family roles defined his life. The real Clarence Thomas is a normal suburban husband and father. Because the hearings had "brought [his] family closer," no one should pity him (Committee 4:184). Twice he used almost identical language to describe himself: "I will go back to my life of talking to my neighbors and cutting my grass and getting a Big Mac at McDonald's and driving my car, and seeing my kid play football. And I will live. I will have my life back" (Committee 4:184: see also Committee 4:257). Thomas would have preferred an assassin's bullet to "this kind of living hell that they have put [him] and [his] family through" (Committee 4:205). The process was destroying everything—his family and his accomplishments. The ordeal had been so traumatic for his family that his mother was "confined to her bed, unable to work and unable to stop crying" (Committee 4:9). He wants his life and, by extension, his family's lives back.

If the senators had given Thomas the respect due him as a patriarch he said, they would have discussed Hill's charges in a closed room. An open hearing signified that Thomas was not an equal. His peers were not protecting him, and if they did not include him as patriarch, then he had lost access to masculine power. Public humiliation marked him as a stereotypical, out-of-control black/male, temporarily unable to assume his grandfather's paternal role. If he could not control himself, he could neither protect his family nor claim the virtue of paternal authority. Loss of status were bring disgrace to his entire family.

Thomas's wife, child, and relatives were not his only family. He portrayed himself as the benevolent, paternal head of his office: "I tend to be the proud father type who sees his special assistants go on and become successful and feels pretty good about it" (Committee 4:182). This comment and others like an appeal to his listeners. Biden discussed his own relationships to his staff in the same terms and then he asked Thomas about his relationship with Hill. "Did you feel a special obligation to look out for her? She was a young woman, so did you say be careful what you do because certain parts of this city are dangerous? Or, you know, you have to be careful who you date, or make sure you call your mother? Or have you called—was his name Gil?" (Committee 4:220).

Hill had a law degree from Yale and a position as an attorney-advisor, yet Thomas did not categorize her as a fellow professional. She was simply one of his family, no different in status from interns or summer staff. Like a good father, Thomas had treated Hill like all of his special assistants. His language was both paternal and paternalistic. Underlying "fatherly" concern is the desire for control and superiority, as evidenced in Thomas's statement: "I view my special assistants as charges of mine. They are students, they are kids of mine, and I have an obligation to them. It is the same way I feel toward interns and individual co-ops or stay-in-school students" (Committee 4:187).

In Hill's case Thomas played the supportive, mentoring father to a somewhat difficult, temperamental child: "I believe that when I have assistants or interns, that I have a personal responsibility for them, as teacher, advisor, not employer. I am the employer, also, but they are my personal charges for whom I have responsibility" (Committee 4:197).

Thomas had encouraged Hill's professional development and had been hopeful about her career (Committee 4:182). He had believed that Hill understood and appreciated his interest in her professional success. He had mentored Hill; she had "sought counsel and advice" from him (Committee 4:168). Thomas did not mention how gratifying these positions were for him. No longer the dependent, Thomas had subordinates beholden to him. He could be the white/male father, like Danforth, to others. He pointed out that Hill had followed him from the Department of Education to the EEOC. This move was during the exact time, November 1981 to February or March 1982, she later alleged he harassed her. As Hill must have known, given her ambitions and self-interest, he said, as a schedule A employee, she could have stayed at the Department of Education. When Hill later decided it was time for her to leave the government and expressed an interest in teaching, he had supported her decision and recommended her for a position. Thomas believed that Hill left Washington, D.C., because she wanted to return to Oklahoma and would have earned the same salary in a position at Oral Roberts University.

Even after she left Washington, D.C., Hill continued to seek Thomas's counsel. She made at least twelve phone calls to him between 1983 and 1990. There could have been more, he said because the only calls recorded were those that required leaving a message. Thomas may also have contacted Hill to see how she was doing, he said. Their contact after her departure continued as it had in Washington—cordial and respectful. Thomas assumed that Hill, like all of his assistants, wanted continued contact with him because he was so supportive of them (Committee 4:183). When a senator asked how Thomas viewed his relationship with them as of August 24, 1991, Thomas replied, "cordial, professional, and that I was very proud of her for all she had done with her life and the things that she had accomplished" (Committee 4:183). Never had Thomas been aware that Hill believed he had done something to change their relationship. He had detected no acrimony from her, his staff, or their mutual friend, Gil Hardy. Hill had never mentioned a problem to other women on his staff or to friends who might have raised the issue with Thomas (Committee 4:157).

Thomas's language revealed a complex and ambivalent attitude rather than mere warm paternal interest in her professional development. Despite portraying himself as a dedicated father to his staff, from the beginning Thomas tried to distance himself from Hill. He described their relationship as "cordial, professional, respectful," all adjectives connoting pleasant but distant. He shifted his designation of her from "friend" to "one of his assistants"—no different from the others and less important than some. Thomas also contradicted himself. Though he was paternal and protective of all of his staff, he claimed to have been less protective of Hill. In response to Biden's question about looking out for Hill, he replied,

I don't recall anything of that nature, Senator. What I was referring to was to make sure that I looked out for her career. . . . The kind of relationship that you are talking about, in your examples, those are the kinds of things I look out for with interns, who are with me during the summer, or individuals who are in co-op programs, those individuals. I have had some who were 19 or 20 years old who I would treat more like my own son or daughter. (Committee 4:220)

Thomas diminished Hill's importance, saying that she worked for him long ago and not for long (Committee 4:264). Not only had he never tried to date Hill, he said, but he could hardly recall her position in the Department of Education in 1981. He did recall that at the Department of Education, they had had a professional but cordial relationship, whereas at the EEOC their relationship was more distant. After he moved to the EEOC, Hill had less access to him and their discussions had been limited (Committee 4:216). On reflection, Thomas recalled that Hill "seemed to have had some difficulty adjusting to this change in her role" (Committee 4:6). Perhaps Hill had wanted more closeness, more personal interest, Thomas implied for the first but not the last time (see, for example, Committee 4:166). Such closeness had never been his wish.

Thomas's paternal and familial language conveyed several important subliminal messages. First, a normal family man could not engage in the perverted behavior Hill had alleged. She must be the abnormal one—a single woman, with no children, subject to all of the suspicions of a "spinster." Such a woman might have been prone to fantasizing and deluding herself about men's interest in her.

Second, Thomas's rage is justified. The hearings had harmed his family, giving him the masculine right and obligation to defend them. In the context of a confirmation hearing, it was appropriate to be emotional, and his reaction affirmed rather than undercut his race/gender status. Hill's temper tantrums, however, were symptoms of her immaturity and instability.

Third, as a member of Thomas's family, he could not have harassed Hill. Furthermore, although he thought of Hill as part of his family, he had never been familiar with her. He had respected the appropriate boundaries and never discussed sex with Hill. He occasionally had driven her home and two or three times had come into her apartment to continue discussions with her. These discussions were always about politics, however. They had occurred in an open area of her apartment, when Hill's roommate also had been there (Committee 4:225). Any sexual behavior toward Hill would have been incest, something normal family men never do.

Finally, Thomas presented himself as a Lear-like father. He was anguished over the betrayal of a well-tended child: "This is a person I have helped at every turn of the road . . . she sought my advice and counsel, as did virtually all the members of my personal staff" (Committee 4:157). Hill's lack of gratitude for his care provided evidence about her, not Thomas's character. Her behavior remained inexplicable and, by implication, inexcusable and monstrous. "I don't know why family members turn on each other. I don't know why a son or daughter or a brother or sister would write some book that destroys a family. I don't know (Committee 4:197). Thomas's pain was a direct measure of how despicable and unreliable Hill was. Hill could never return to the Senate hearing like a prodigal son because the senators could empathize with Thomas's pain.

CHAPTER SEVEN

"This Is All Shakespeare": Doggett and the Transformation of Tragedy into Farce

The second hearing posed the minor puzzle of why the senators would listen to John Doggett for such a long time. Doggett was an acquaintance of both Thomas and Hill. He was a third-year student when Thomas entered Yale Law School. The three associated with the small group of black Yale graduates in Washington, D.C. Doggett volunteered to share with the committee his impressions of Hill. Why the senators would take seriously Doggett's testimony is unclear. Biden characterized Doggett's testimony as requiring a "leap of faith or ego" (Committee 4:559). Doggett admitted he had had very little contact with Hill, but he offered an analysis of Hill's mental state and character based on three instances that occurred eight or nine years previously over a period of eighteen months: "So in those three instances— my own personal experience, a statement by a business school colleague and friend of mine, and my one observation about Anita Hill and Clarence Thomas back, I believe, 1982, there is a consistency in a perception of something that did not exist" (Committee 4:572). Despite Doggett's admission and the "leap of faith" his testimony required, many on the committee took him quite seriously. Spector, for example, thanked him for his "very powerful" testimony (Committee 4:573).

Although Doggett had had very little direct interaction with Hill, he felt competent to analyze her mental health and character. He could provide solid evidence of her propensity to fantasize, undermining the credibility of her charges; however, he saw no contradiction in basing his testimony on intuition. "I was going on a gut sense, on male intuition" (Committee 4:569). When asked if he had personal knowledge (apart from opinion) that could substantiate Hill's lack of credibility, Doggett admitted that he had "no way of knowing" (Committee 4:583).

Doggett was reminiscent of Shakespeare's Falstaff or a chorus member in a classical Greek play. He served as a foil or an absurd character who illuminates the whole. The senators allowed him to proceed while distancing themselves. This tactic allowed them to claim a more rational masculinity. Like the chorus in a Greek drama, Doggett articulated undisguised sentiments that for various reasons other players could not. He revealed debasing attitudes toward women, especially Hill, as well as grandiose ideas about masculine power. This power included knowing women's unspoken thoughts through superior masculine intution. Although he admitted "I am not a psychiatrist, I am not an expert, just a man" (Committee 4:559), his masculinity lent him expertise.

Through Doggett, the senators reinforced the race/gender bonding already under way. Denigrating women was an important element of this bond, but Doggett's presence the gave the senators an opportunity to disavow it. Doggett's extreme and undisguised statement of these ideas provided them with deniability. They appeared fair and objective whereas he looked like a fool.

Doggett also offered a near-parody of Thomas's life story. Doggett's efforts and emotions were an uncanny echo of Thomas's, but Doggett presented them so broadly that he reduced them to farce. Doggett also served Thomas by epitomizing race/gender stereotypes. He was a race/gender jester, the identify onto which the senators could project their male/Africanist fantasies. In contrast to Doggett, Thomas was so refined that he escaped this categorization. The senators encouraged Doggett to occupy the black/male position so Thomas could avoid it. Thomas was anti-Doggett, and real men were not like Doggett. Doggett's testimony kept fantasies about the male/Africanist presence intact and proved that exception.

This use of Doggett benefited everyone except Hill. For reinforcing the organization of race/gender, Doggett gained partial entry into the world of powerful white/males. Entry to this world comes with a price. Existing race/gender arrangements cannot accommodate too many exceptions because their weight would eventually destroy the structure. Doggett did not disturb dominant ideas about white/male subjectivity and, by listening to him, the senators maintained race/gender dominance.

Doggett offered himself as a witness because he had crucial, even probative, evidence about Hill's mental state and character. This evidence had direct bearing on her credibility and Thomas's innocence. As Thomas had, he established his credibility be telling his life story—constructing his own character defense before attacking Hill. Although he, like Thomas, was saddened that people were "throwing mud," he believed that either Thomas or Hill had "to be destroyed if the nation [were] to be saved" (Committee 4:431). Like Thomas, Doggett had come from a poor background and struggled against prejudice. Education had provided the opportunity for success. He had attended Yale Law School and later Harvard Business School. Also like Thomas, he insisted that he had suffered from racism but never benefited from affirmative action.

He, too, expected to be attacked for both his independence and his appearance before the committee: "I knew when I put my information into the ring that I was saying I am open season and people are going to shoot at me (Committee 4:565). His status as an attorney and businessman rendered him, like Thomas, vulnerable to efforts to destroy all uppity blacks. He recalled Thomas telling him, "These people are going to shoot at me. I have a target on my back. It is one of my jobs to make sure that I am not going to be the black in the Reagan Administration who gets tarred and feathered" (Committee 4:575). This statement was a warning to any independent black man, and Doggett took it seriously. As a black man, he too was vulnerable to "have something like this [the use of sexual charges to undermine his credibility] crawl out from under a rock" (Committee 4:566).

But Doggett did not care if he were attacked. Like Thomas, he was not intimidated by bullies: "I have information I think the committee needs to hear. If they feel it is relevant enough for me to be here, I will be here and I will take whatever occurs" (Committee 4:566). Despite the vulnerability he would risk, he was willing to sacrifice himself for the nation's well-being. This willingness evidenced his moral superiority, masculine strength, and dedication to truth.

Doggett discussed his few brief encounters with Hill. He had observed her at parties for black graduates of Yale Law School. Doggett had seen her once while jogging and talk with her briefly then. Once he had run into her while visiting Thomas, and he had seen her for the last time at her going-away party before she left for Oklahoma. Like Thomas's his memories of Hill were simultaneously detailed and blurred. Both men used their fading memories to disavow their negative implications about Hill. For example, Doggett cited as a main source of evidence mutual but separate attendance at events for black Yale Law graduates. All these parties Doggett said, he had "observed from a distance—and I am not a psychiatrist, I am not an expert, just a man—Anita Hill attempting to be friendly with men, engage them in conversation, initiate conversation, elongate conversations, and people talking with her and eventually going away" (Committee 4:559).

Doggett concluded from his observations that Hill had a pattern of hitting on men. She had trouble interesting men and easily felt rejected. She lacked the social skills to attract a man and was probably continually frustrated in her efforts: "I never saw any of those conversations result in people continuing to talk with her . . . When somebody is trying to, to use the terminology, 'hit on somebody,' and the result is people walk away, and you see that happen more than one time, it leads you to believe, Senator, that maybe something is not working" (Committee 4:577).

Despite this detailed account, however, when Biden asked whether Doggett could name the men Hill approached, Doggett said no. The parties had occurred eight or nine years ago. He then blamed Hill for his memory loss: "If she had filed a sexual harassment charge then, he could have" (Committee 4:560). He did, however, remember that "The first time I met Anita Hill I sensed she was interested in knowing me better and I was not interested in getting to know Anita Hill. And based on my experience as a black male in this town, I did everything I could to try not to give her any indication that I was interested in her" (Committee 4:555).

Like Thomas, he had intended his relationship with Hill to be cordial, professional, and supportive: "I tried to make it very clear that although I respected her as a person and as a fellow alumnus of Yale Law School, and as somebody I thought was very decent, the only relationship I was interested in was a professional relationship" (Committee 4:555). He, too, felt responsible to Hill because Gil Hardy was his friend and he saw her as part of his family:

The group of black Yale Law School graduates is a very small, a very close, and a very special group and it is like a family. Gil Hardy, the man who introduced Anita to Clarence Thomas, was one of the leaders of that group. We did what we could to be as supportive as possible. Senator, I graduated in 1972. She graduated in 1980. She was significantly younger than me, she seemed to be lonely in this town. I was not going to try to make this woman feel that I was not going to be straightforward with her as a professional. There have been other women who have made it very clear to me that they have been interested in me and I have said, I am not interested. Anita Hill did nothing to deserve me to slam the door in her face. She was one of the Yale Law School black fraternity and there are very few of them, Senator. (Committee 4:560)

Despite this patronizing statement about family loyalty, Doggett specified nothing in particular that he had ever done for Hill—other than avoid her invitation to have dinner together. The paucity of his encounters with her made it unclear how he could have ever transmitted this information or support. Before her going-away party, Doggett had had two brief direct exchanges with Hill. One occurred when he went to see Thomas, and the supposed solidarity of Yale Law School graduates had not operated: "As I went into his outer office, Anita Hill happened to walk by and she tried to stop me and engage me in conversation and acted as though she thought that since we were all black Yale Law School graduates, I should say, well, let's go in and talk with Clarence, which I did not" (Committee 4:560). Instead, Doggett offered this encounter as evidence that Hill had been prone to respond to disappointment by fantasizing about nonexistent familiarity or status. The incident also suggested that Hill was frustrated by her exclusion from Thomas's inner circle. The "look on Anita Hill's face" when Doggett did not invite her to come and talk to Thomas revealed her frustration (Committee 4:577).

Doggett's brief encounter when he jogged by her apartment led to a five- or ten-minute conversation. Doggett could not remember "exactly how long it was. It is a long time ago" (Committee 4:577). He did remember, however, that he had wanted to keep running. Doggett had stopped to be courteous. His obligation to Hardy and other members of their "fraternity" required such behavior. Doggett had been certain that Hill wanted to prolong the conversation, as with the men at the graduation parties. "The reason we continued to talk was because she wanted me to continue to talk. That is action on her part, sir" (Committee 4:560). He said that he had determined from Hill's body language and questions that she was interested in him (Committee 4:577). During this conversation, Hill suggested that because they were neighbors, perhaps they could have dinner. Doggett said he later checked his calendar and asked about dinner that Tuesday. Hill was to have gotten back to him with a response but the plans fell through. Evidently, each had thought the other should confirm the plans. Hill had called Doggett, inquiring about what had happened. According to Doggett, there had been an awkward pause. He had not been interested so he had not suggested another date (Committee 4:555). Doggett assumed that Hill had been deeply disappointed and later exacted revenge at her going-away party.

Doggett had not seen Hill again until this party. There she had "dropped a bombshell" on him (Committee 4:555). As she had betrayed Thomas, Hill suddenly lodged irrational charges of a sexual nature against Doggett. Her comments at the going-away party "seemed to be very, very serious, and that is how I took them" (Committee 4:584). Hill had approached Doggett and, according to Doggett, said, "I'm very disappointed in you. You really shouldn't lead women on, or lead women on and then let them down" (Committee 4:554–555). Doggett had felt stunned and betrayed. Her comment was "totally inappropriate, given everything [he had] tried to do to be a supportive, older, upper classman, part of the Yale Law School group" (Committee 4:572).

Doggett believed that this encounter was highly significant and revealing of Hill's character. He "came away from her 'going-away' party feeling that she was somewhat unstable and that in my case she had fantasized about my being interested in her romantically" (Committee 4:554). Hill's fantasies about Doggett's interest in her were presented as evidence of her difficulty in accepting male rejection. Doggett concluded from this experience that Hill's allegations about Thomas were simply "another example of her ability to fabricate the idea that someone was interested in her when in fact no such interest existed" (Committee 4:554).

Although all of these events were supposedly Hill's fantasies, Doggett insisted on the enormity of Hill's capacity for damage. No one disputed his characterization of her statement as a "bombshell." He appeared to equate the trauma this remark caused him with the spiritual death Thomas had described (Committee 4:558). The committee permitted him to play the role of a sexual harassment victim. They did not question his description or his account of the remark's impact. Doggett had confirmed Hill's position as harasser as well as the innocence of her targets. None of the senators suggested that flirting at a party might have a different valence and consequences than sexual inuendo in a workplace. They did not discuss the structural differences between two people at a party and an employee and her boss.

Doggett offered another example of Hill's alleged propensity to fantasize. He said that he could establish a pattern of Hill's exaggerated interest in men. Doggett had been friendly with John Carr, a man Hill claimed she dated. According to Doggett, however, Carr had never mentioned dating Hill or any discussions with Hill about her alleged problems with Thomas (Committee 4:434). He and Carr had been such good friends, he said, that had Hill's claims been true, Carr would have discussed them with Doggett. Carr had a different view. When Biden asked him, "Did you go out alone with her from time to time?" Carr replied, "Yes, I would characterize it that we met, we dated, and the bulk of our relationship was on the telephone getting to know one another. . . . I guess I would say we didn't get but so far" (Committee 4:282). This relationship occurred in 1982–1983, during the time when Hill worked for Thomas. Carr said that during one phone conversation Hill had seemed upset. She had admitted reluctantly that she was upset because "her boss was making sexual advances toward her" (Committee 4:274). No one addressed the discrepancies between Doggett's and Carr's testimonies.

Although some disagreed about how to interpret Hill's behavior outside of work, no one seemed to consider it irrelevant. The committee appeared to consider any facet of Hill's life open to analysis. Biden told Doggett, "I think your judgment about women is not so hot, whether or not people fantasize or don't. You and I disagree on that" (Committee 4:568). Biden did not, however, disagree that dating and Hill's social behavior were relevant. The senators discussed these topics repeatedly, and Doggett assumed they were on shared terrain. At one point, he said, "I don't know about you, gentlemen," but he had found Washington, D.C., a difficult place for single people (Committee 4:556). Biden admitted to some difficulty with contemporary phrases used to describe interactions between men and women. He told the committee that his sons, twenty-one and twenty-two years old, believed that he was out of it. Brown also admitted that "It has been some time since [he had] been an unmarried person, so [he was] not sure [he was] an expert on this point." He did suggest that "the conversation that took place seemed to me could be nothing more than someone flirting with you" (Committee 4:583). Doggett rejected this suggestion because Hill had "seemed very upset" (Committee 4:557). He had "never perceived Anita to be flirting . . . [he] perceived her to, as a man, be indicating that if [he] was interested in getting to know her better that she would be interested" (Committee 4:584). Biden asked whether Doggett had told Hill to never call again. Although according to Doggett the only time Hill had ever mentioned his letting her down was at the going-away party, Doggett replied, "I sure wish I had" (Committee 4:556).

Doggett also adopted Thomas's aggressively innocent and victimized stance. Metzenbaum questioned Doggett about a charge that Doggett had sexually harassed a young temporary employee at work. Metzenbaum read portions of a transcript that included senatorial staffers questioning Doggett about the employee. Doggett's response, like Thomas's, equated his own integrity with the nation's: "Senator, your comments about this document are one of the reasons that our process of government is falling apart" (Committee 4:564). Initially he claimed that he did not remember the person who made the allegations (Committee 4:567); however, he had remembered that she was nineteen years old and white (Committee 4:564). He used this information to prove that he would never have harassed her. As a black man, he was too savvy about political history to sexually approach a white woman. He offers a defense parallel to Thomas's: "Doing what [Hill] alleges that he did with her was a prescription for instant death.

Clarence is not a fool" (Committee 4:573). The discussion again erased Hill's race/gender. Harassment of a black/female would not have resulted in instant death for any male.

Metzenbaum asked Doggett how he could know that an accuser he did not remember was nineteen years old and white. Doggett equivocated and then contradicted himself: "It has been eight or nine years and I, even I, can forget people" (Committee 4:569). Then, like Thomas, he took the offensive and claimed he had been abused. Doggett, not his accuser, was the victim of unwarranted attacks. He drew a parallel between Thomas's situation and his own: "I demand the right to clear my name, sir. I have been trashed for no reason by somebody who does not even have the basic facts right. This is what is going on with Clarence Thomas, and now I, another person coming up, has had a 'witness' fabricated at the last moment to try to keep me from testifying" (Committee 4:565).

Doggett also said that he "had just started a relationship with an attorney, a very intense relationship" (Committee 4:567). Despite Doggett's supposed expertise on sexual harassment, his implication, like Thomas's, was that sexual harassment is about sex, rather than power. Hill fantasized, he implied, because she was unstable, sexually frustrated, and inept; Doggett could not sexually harass because he was none of those things. Furthermore, unlike mentally unstable women who cannot distinguish fantasy from reality, men are rational. Even in sexual matters, they evaluate costs and benefits. They choose the benefits of access to power over momentary sexual gratification, unless, perhaps, a woman is worth the risk. To sacrifice the benefits of power, a woman would have to be the equivalent of Helen of Troy. Doggett believed he had given the ultimate defense and condemnation of his accuser and Thomas's when he described both women as fundamentally lacking. They were not sexually alluring enough for men to forfeit access to power: "Quite frankly, Anita Hill is not worth that type of risk" (Committee 4:573).

Doggett also suggested that his accuser had sexually harassed the nation. He represented decency, and the committee should treat him as its ally: "All I can say is that I expected somebody to do something like this because that is what this process has become, and one of the reasons I am here is to work with you gentlemen to try to take the public process back into the pale of propriety" (Committee 4:567).

Doggett's language was quite suggestive. The phrase "pale of propriety" suggests racial images. Like Thomas, Doggett appealed to male solidarity—men must close ranks against the potentially disruptive threats of hysterical women who seek to exploit men's sexual vulnerabilities. If the agents of order were black/males and if their inclusion in the networks of power restored race/gender dominance, he implied, then they should be allowed within the pale (thereby paleing them in the process).

Despite Doggett's willingness to help destroy Hill, Doggett—like Thomas—presented himself as a champion of women. He often hired women and had "a very clear, long record of commitment, sensitivity, and support for women having the greatest role possible" (Committee 4:568). Like Thomas, Hatch, and Simpson, however, he worried about the alleged victims using sexual harassment policies to victimize others, especially men:

Doggett: I am afraid that the outlandish allegations of Anita Hill are going to result in us feeling that it is inappropriate for us to be human beings with people if they happen to be women. Nobody would ever question me if I put my hand around this man, who I have never met.
Biden: He might.
Doggett: Well, maybe he would. But I hope we don't get to the point where if anybody by any way, accidentally or purposely, innocently touches somebody of the opposite sex, that becomes sexual harassment. (Committee 4:568)

This statement may have been an indirect reply to the charges against him, but it also suggested that women are prone to misinterpret men's innocent gestures. It is unwise, he implied, to give women the opportunity through the law to turn fantasy into legal charges. Like affirmative action, sexual harassment policies are dangerous because they make it possible for self-defined victims to usurp power. These subordinates then can use power to redefine the behaviors of dominant others. They can undermine existing hierarchies of control and privilege. Men can defend themselves against each other, but they may be helpless against female irrationality.

The political context and culturally sanctioned attitudes that Doggett's testimony revealed are not amusing. Doggett described an important network of ideas and authority that enable men to enjoy, obfuscate, and disavow the potent interactions between sex and power. A benefit of power is participating in the traffic in women. The pleasure of domination animates, permits, and reproduces this structure. Sexual harassment is one example of it.

Doggett's testimony revealed more than a shared grammar of masculinity. It also demonstrated one way to trump some contradictions of abstract individualism. Each individual deserves fair and objective treatment, yet abstract individualism is generated by and depends on race/gender solidarity. Networks of power must operate to sustain existing relations of domination without appearing to do so. When existing hierarchies are threatened, order must be restored without appearing to favor anyone. Paradoxically, one way that conflict between equal treatment and maintained hierarchy is resolved is through commitment to fairness. Only individuals must be treated fairly, and some people, for example fantasizing women, cannot function as individuals. Therefore, they deserve different treatment.

The committee constructed Hill as incapable of telling the truth. It did not have to endorse the proposition that Thomas was telling the truth or that Hill was lying. Thomas's word had not been pitted against an individual as rational as he was. Hill, prone to fantasy like many women, could not distinguish truth from lie. Hill was not lying, Spector said; he was just fantasizing (Committee 4:570–571). Doggett suggested that Hill believed what she charged, although "the things she was saying in my mind were absolutely, totally beyond the pale of reality" (Committee 4:573). Female irrationality marks a race/gender boundary. Although men may make leaps of ego, they are not prone to fantasy. The committee did not treat Doggett as an interesting example of how one's own mental processes can be split off, denied, or projected onto subordinated others, and they did not ask Doggett about his propensity to fantasize, even when he made huge leaps based on what he called "male intuition." For example, Leahy said that Hill claimed to hardly remember Doggett. Doggett disagreed: "I looked at Anita Hill's face when you folks mentioned my name. She remembers me, Senator. I assure you of that" (Committee 4:576). Leahy asked, "Based on such minimal contacts with Professor Hill, how could you conclude that she had fantasies about your sexual interest in her, or do you just feel that you have some kind of natural irresistibility?" Doggett replied that his "wife says [he does]" (Committee 4:576). In this statement, Doggett showed how he could disavow his narcissism and fantasizing by placing them in another female. Hill, not Doggett, overestimated had sexual attractiveness. Another woman testifies to the truth of his. He was sexually successful; she was not.

Hill, a subject who occupied two of the least privileged positions in contemporary U. S. politics (black/woman) was positioned as a threat to the nation's integrity. Only fraternity could restore civility and decency to the public world, and this heroic task might require the provisional admission of some black/males into the pale of propriety. In moments of such danger, their inclusion is worth the risk. Some subordinates had already made considerable effort to signify their loyalty. When the nation is at war, it is willing to arm reliable black/males and induct them into the military. The situation in 1991 was similar. The fate of the nation was believed to be at stake. As Kohl said,

> I would like to say to Judge Thomas and to all of us who are here today and listening that this is obviously not what America ought to be. And while we want to get to the truth in this particular case, the truth will be well-served if all of us stop and think long and hard about what we are doing to our nation. We simply have to restore civility and decency to the public debate. (Committee 4:264)

Affirming Thomas's nomination signified restoration of public order as well as the hierarchies and stories that support it. America could again dream in peace.

Why Race/Gender Domination Persists:
The Necessary Failures of Abstract
Individualism and Identity Politics

DeConcini: The founding fathers . . . did not do a perfect job. It
took a long time before we finally did some of the things we should
have done earlier on (Committee 1:195)

   Kennedy: Millions of our fellow citizens are still left out and behind because of unacceptable conditions of discrimination based on
race, sex, age, disability, and other forms of bigotry that continue to
plague our society. (Committee 1:36)

Did the Thomas hearings restore public order? Can the United States
again dream in peace? Can the American dream be realized without
reproduction of the inequalities on which it has depended? The
hearings showed that without changing the normative subject of
American politics—abstract individualism—race/gender domination will persist. The hearings did not change the costs of order—reinforcing dominance and the narratives that support it. Given the
rapid demographic shifts in the United States and the determined resistance of subordinates to their position order is neither secure nor
tranquil. As the hearings did show, however, a predominant way of
resisting inequality—identity politics—is equally problematic. Like
abstract individualism, identity politics also depends on faulty notions of subjectivity. It cannot produce the liberatory results its advocates intend.

   Clarence Thomas was both imprisoned by and a manipulator of the
politics of contemporary subjectivity. The main approaches of this
type of politics and their defects were evident in Thomas's shifting
strategies. He swung between abstract individualism and identity
politics. His first approach was to claim entitlement to the moral

weight of the self-made individual—the Horatio Alger story. Thomas's history served as proof of his good character and worthiness, yet race/gender interrupted and particularized his story. Under attack, Thomas resorted to identity politics, redefining himself as a race victim and evoking the guilt of white/male Americans who were aware of the undelivered promises of equal opportunity. His second strategy undermined his claim to the first, the supposed neutrality of abstract individualism. Identity politics reduced his moral status. His successes were no longer his own but rather were representative of a less privileged and perhaps inferior group. Moreover, identity politics also undermined the coherence and plausibility of the senators' claim to abstract individualism. The metaphor of lynching reminded Thomas's examiners that they too had a collective race/gender. Historically, only white/males have enjoyed the full privileges of individualism—fairness, equality, and protection under the law. By admitting Thomas into their circle, however, the senators regained their status and redeemed the promise of equal opportunity. They resuscitated the abstract individual.

The unsatisfying outcome of the hearings showed that neither abstract individualism nor identity politics can be the basis of even a shadow of the American dream. Rather than producing tranquility, the existing hierarchies often generate hatred. Rarely do we think of our communities as bound by hatred. In fact, the resurgence of "communitarian" writings ignores these bonds altogether.[1] At least in American history, however, hatred has been an important source of solidarity. Hatred ties people together in ways that they cannot consciously acknowledge. It generates a desire to destroy others who affect one's own fate. As W. Ronald D. Fairbairn argues; the bonds of shared hatred are among the most difficult to break.[2]

Why is hatred a recurring feature of American politics? Part of the answer lies in maintaining our founding identity. Incorporating the history of race relations, even coded as black people's experience with segregation, would destabilize the foundation. The tensions of race relations undermine beliefs in America's special goodness, in white innocence, and in the neutrality of the law. The abstract individual is a defense against acknowledging the inescapable race/gender specificity of all modern subjects. The result of these race/gender instabilities is heightened levels of public and subjective anxiety and race/gender tension.

Abstract individualism encourages the development of sado-masochistic relationships within and among subjects. David Theo Goldberg said, "Negating others, denigrating them, becomes in part also self-negation and self-denigration."[3] Subordinate others may incorporate some of these negativities into their own self-assessments. They, too, may violate themselves and develop powerful self-hatred. One hates oneself for being mutilated by one's own actions and those of others. Identifying with the wounding other is both painful and shaming.[4] However longed for, no amount of retribution or reparation fully repairs such damage. Rage feeds on itself and produces some of the violence that is so pervasive in contemporary social relations.

Paradoxically, despite the destructiveness of race/gender, the need for it may intensify as the U.S. population becomes increasingly racially diverse. Toni Morrison wrote, "As a metaphor for transacting the whole process of Americanization, while burying its particular racial ingredients, this Africanist presence may be something the United States cannot do without. Deep within the word 'American' is its association with race. American means white."[5] A coherent sense of American citizenship may require the outsider within; plurality without hierarchy has never been the American way because someone must bear the race/gender particularity masked by abstract individualism. This paradox makes it all the more vital to explore the links between abstract individualism and race/gender dominance.

This chapter develops the broad and theoretical implications of the Thomas hearings. The hearings showed that more just politics require transforming our normative ideas of subjectivity and developing new political practices. These practices will resist major tenets of abstract individualism and identity politics, including the dominant and some subordinate ideas about race/gender. I propose replacing politics based on homogeneous subjects—abstract individuals or concrete race/gender ones—with "object-centered" practices. The overlapping desires of complex subjects would generate these objects. Multiplicity, rather than homogeneity, would be a defining quality of these emerging "diasporian" subjects. The political practices of these subjects may be less tranquil, because they will have conflicting desires and loyalties, but they will also depend far less on hatred.

THE NORMATIVE AMERICAN SUBJECT: ABSTRACT INDIVIDUALISM AS A MANIC DEFENSE

In *The Racial Contract,* Charles W. Mills wrote,

One could say then, as a general rule, that *white misunderstanding, misrepresentation, evasion, and self-deception on matters related to race* are among the most pervasive mental phenomena of the past few hundred years, a cognitive and moral economy psychically required for conquest, colonization, and enslavement. And these phenomena are in no way *accidental,* but *prescribed* by the terms of the Racial Contract, which requires a certain schedule of structured blindnesses and opacities in order to establish and maintain the white polity.[6]

In the Thomas hearings, as elsewhere, abstract individualism functioned as a manic defense. Manic defenses enable the subject to ward off aspects of subjectivity that produce anxiety or that disorganize identity. By employing this defense, the subject fantasizes the disappearance of particular aspects of his or her world. Similarly, in the Thomas hearings and American politics more generally, abstract individualism permits some subjects to disavow their race/gender positions.

John Rawls's account of the "veil of ignorance" offers an unintended but literal example of how abstract individualism operates as a manic defense.[7] Before liberal citizens establish their governing principles, they must deliberately block all knowledge of their social construction. This original position is necessary because one can take up others' viewpoints only if one fully erases one's own. Otherwise, alternate positions could not be adopted accurately. One's own interests would distort the perceptions of alternatives. Contrary to Rawls's claims, however, this erasure does not ensure rational deliberation. The erasure of social construction is an illusion; the veil of ignorance blinds those who operate behind it to their own determinants. Behind the veil, subjects can sustain a fantasy that they are the masters of— rather than formed by—their social history. The veil allows subjects to delude themselves and to collude with others who also imagine themselves as veiled. In their ignorance, they mistake defensively constructed ideas for generally applicable principles of justice.

As Thomas's narrative showed, belief in the abstract individual is appealing to everyone, not just dominant groups. For subordinates, the idea is a defense against the despair of living within race/gender asymmetries. It works as a magic totem to ward off the anxiety that domination may be inescapable.[8] If all persons can become "individuals" and privilege is a function of individual virtues, then race/gender will neither restrict nor expand anyone's life chances. If either of these beliefs is unfounded, however, then oppression will not end without major social transformations. Radical shifts of cultural, economic, and political power will be necessary. The prognosis for the oppressed is grim because a major transformation is not in everyone's immediate interest.

The Subject of Identity Politics

Identity politics is the complementary opposite of abstract individualism. Both are products of the same political logic. "Minority" racial and abstract individual identities are equally homogeneous. Dominant and subordinate subjects derive their identities from uniformity—sameness. We are defined either by a particular identity or by an absolute lack of one. In the terms of the Thomas hearings, we can be either homogeneous victims of oppression or reflective, rational legislators who articulate universalized principles. Liberalism requires that claims to justice must be made on the basis of principles that apply to and are recognized by all—dominant and subordinate groups. Injustice is the *uniform* oppression of a homogeneous group. When these positions are believed to be isolated and disconnected, the victim cannot also be the victimizer. People with certain race/gender identities are, by definition, victims, incapable of oppressing others. This paradigm dictates that racial differences are absolute and rigidly bounded. A certain skin color results in a delimited and predictable set of experiences and interests, and these experiences will necessarily cause one to have certain ideas and moral commitments.

Subordinate groups who adopt identity politics stake their hopes of emancipation on the existence of uniform minority subjects. They simply resist the dominant group's explanation for, or understanding of, the subjects' difference. Identity politics has two possible moves— transvaluation or victimization. The former is a process of reversing the normative connotations of the agreed-upon differences. The process transforms the negative connotations into positive ones; for example, black is renamed beautiful. The latter move is victimization—a negative assertion of sameness. Subordinates assert they are identical to the dominant. Their position is uniformly inferior only because the dominant oppress all subordinates in same way. If this oppression were eliminated, the difference would disappear.

Some pan-Africanist, Afro-centrist, and feminist political practices engage in transvaluation. For example, some feminists accept the traditional idea that women are more nurturing than men. They claim, however, that this sensitivity provides the basis for a different kind of politics, one grounded in an ethics of caring. This kind of politics is as good as, if not better than, traditional, aggressive "male" politics, they assert. Similarly, pan-Africanists claim that shared origins (for example, African roots) produce uniform, unique cultural/subjective attributes. The glories of an African heritage warrant the superiority of an African American identity. Sharing this heritage invariably gives rise to collective demands that reflect a common good. Returning to one's roots is a way to overcome domination.

Alternatively, subordinates may claim that victimization accounts for their inability to achieve sameness. Their claim may produce some short-term gains; however, its costs far outweigh the gains. Self-described victimization is self-destructive and double-edged; it locates the subject as a victim, not an agent, of history. The social and psychological relationships of victimization reproduce inequality. Whereas victimization might be grounds for social restitution, it is a poor basis for equality or self-respect. The victimized are viewed as less competent than those who are not victimized. Others regard victims with a mixture of guilt and contempt. Furthermore, victims view their victimizers with hatred and helplessness, and they reject any agency, fearing it will absolve the victimizers of responsibility. Endless political stasis results from these victim/victimizer positions. Guilt produces bad faith, and an identity as a victimizer paradoxically relieves one of concrete, practical responsibility. Despite sometimes harming themselves or other oppressed subjects, victims absolve themselves of complicity in relationships of domination. Assigning responsibility is a zero-sum game; neither victim nor victimizer can work out accountability. The victimization process requires that the victimizer be totally guilty and the victim totally innocent. Victimizers naturally reject total guilt, and blame the subordinate exclusively, thus absolving themselves of any responsibility.

Changing the Subject: Rethinking Race/Gender

Subordinates believe they can use identity politics to resist dominance; however, this approach results in deeper entrapment in oppressive race/gender relationships. Adopting either transvaluation or victimization entails acceptance of the dominant groups' power to construct norms and categories. Identity politics does not challenge the arbitrary division of subjects into race/gender categories. Advocates of identity politics do not question the dominant narrative in which race/gender emerges as a social fact. Instead, identity politics produces a continuing investment in the effects of domination—race/gender-based identities and the belief that only uniform subjects deserve justice. To weaken domination, we need to think about subjectivity in different ways.

Reconsidering subjectivity requires going beyond the naturalized perspectives of race/gender that characterize both abstract individualism and identity politics. The inadequacy of dominant and subordinate ideas about race/gender reflect the investment by some in sustaining current hierarchies. Biology, anthropology, and history all make readily available information that undercuts race/gender as portrayed by abstract individualism and identity politics.

An alternative understanding of race/gender requires that we relocate all subjects within race/gender. Insisting that race/gender shapes all contemporary subjects implies, incorrectly, that race/gender is inescapable. All social constructs, including race/gender, reflect the practices of the subjects who are formed through them. These practices and race/gender itself are heterogeneous and unstable; therefore, it is possible for subjects individually and collectively to resist, transmute, or even obliterate it.

Although understanding race/gender is difficult, it does have an identifiable morphology in the contemporary United States.[9] A pair of negatives, one singular and one double, forms the structure. These negatives are asymmetric in social value and power, but the existence and meaning of each depend on the other. Placement within the negatives determines each subject's race/gender.

The double negative is not-not white. Purity requires the existence of the impure; only by contrast can purity be meaningful. White is the pure, the absence of color, unraced. Whiteness requires the absence of all raced (non-white) blood.[10] Raced subjects include everyone who does not fit into this category; they are persons of color.

The single negative is not-male. Not-male subjects attain rank according to their approximation to the norm (male-ness). White, heterosexual males define full masculinity, the normative position. White/males are not, however, considered to be gendered; women are "the sex" and constrained by their condition. The putative absence of race/gender in white/males enables them to assume abstract individualism. Raced and gay males are deficient, but they still have some claim to masculinity; females are not-males and utterly lacking. Class status may entitle one to privileges within a race/gender position and perhaps even across it; however, even considerable economic power and social status cannot obliterate all of the effects of subordinate race/gender positions.[11] Within femininity, a spectrum also exists: white, heterosexual females are the ideal, whereas lesbians and raced females are variously defective. Once race and sexuality are taken seriously, gender can no longer be defined as a simple, binary opposition composed only of the two categories of man and woman.

Although race/gender is socially constructed and contestable, for contemporary American subjects it is neither voluntary nor completely conscious. It is subject to change, but it also forms us. Some of its effects are so pervasive that they exceed our capacity for recognition and action. For the individual subject, race/gender is a command and a previously assigned boundary. Unless contemporary Americans locate ourselves within race/gender, we cannot become socially recognized or recognizable. Each subject's sense of personal position requires the simultaneous invention of the other. For example, to construct white/male subjectivity, one must imagine and then reject several positions: I am not a white/woman because they are x, and I am q. I am not a black/male, because they are y, and I am z.

For white women and men, race/gender others are sites onto which problematic aspects of their own desires, especially those that undercut socially acceptable race/gender identities, are projected. Through this process of projection, whites construct what Toni Morrison calls the "Africanist presence," an imaginary being whites use to think about themselves in different ways.[12] This construct is constantly reworked and acquires multiple, contradictory valences. The other can be an object of envy, idealization, or denigration. Morrison says that it can represent a "marker and vehicle for illegal sexuality, fear of madness, expulsion, self-loathing."[13] Simultaneously, a fantasized black culture is often the object of white subjects' envy or imaginary emulation. Black culture may be envisioned as hip and ultra-urbane behavior. It is the projected site of a desire to transgress the boring conformity of white, suburban, middle-class normality.

The Africanist presence enables white subjects to sort and contain anxieties about sexuality.[14] For example, projecting sexuality onto race/gender others reinforces the recurring myth of true (desexualized) womanhood. Masculinity is dependent upon and shaped by notions of sexual prowess and competition over heterosexual performance. White/males can manage some of their anxieties about masculinity through fantasies about subordinate men. In these fantasies, the race/gender other is so sexually superior that he becomes an animal and, paradoxically, is no longer competition. The race/gender other defines the limit on expectations by both masculine peers and fully human women.

Although race/gender shapes all contemporary Americans, not all subjects possess equal power. Dominant groups possess the power to define others as different and inferior. The other's deficiencies justify the dominant's privilege. Subordinate groups resist and try to redefine the positions, but dominant subjects often succeed in reproducing the power structures that support their positions. Most accounts of race/gender delineate its horrifying effects on subordinates. Whereas these descriptions are necessary, the impact of exercising domination on the dominant is rarely discussed. Analyzing this effect requires belief in the formative effects of race/gender on everyone and acknowledgment of the determining force of the Africanist presence in white imagination.

Positing autonomous white and black histories is erroneous. Indeed, as Paul Gilroy writes, the "modern cultural history of blacks in the modern world has a great bearing on ideas of what the West was and is today."[15] Rethinking history requires awakening from the amnesia of the dominant race/gender regarding the centrality of slavery in modern history. Much of U. S. history would be taught quite differently from slaves' perspectives. Their viewpoints would both integrate brutality and terror into contemporary American self-understandings and alter the meaning of emancipation as well as the view of history as progressive. The slaves' perspectives would complicate belief in a singular historical subject and the intrinsic emancipatory potential of liberal states. One would have to accept as constitutional, rather than accidental, the "foundational ethnocentrism in which these have all tended to be anchored."[16]

Rethinking U. S. cultural history is not encouraged by the dominant race/gender. As the Thomas hearings showed, white Americans have hardly begun to grapple with the legacy of slavery. Senator Spector was an exception to this rule. He disagreed with Hatch's characterization of bigotry as unAmerican. Instead, he reluctantly agreed with a conclusion Thomas once supported. Thomas had said, "the Dred Scott decision, which upheld slavery, . . . put a backdrop of racism and discrimination which are deeply rooted in the history of the

United States and remain even to the present time" (Committee 1:72). Spector believed that unfortunately Thomas's statement about racism and discrimination was accurate. Most of the senators, however, took the dominant approach, assigning slavery to "black" history. As Gilroy wrote, "If perceived as relevant at all, the history of slavery is somehow assigned to blacks. It becomes our special property rather than a part of the ethical and intellectual heritage of the West as a whole."[17]

Slavery played an essential, often overlooked, role in shaping contemporary ideas about subjectivity. Slavery provided not only labor and wealth but also the defining limit against which modern American subjects can comprehend their own freedom.[18] In the United States, race/gendered understandings of society and subjectivity evolved along with slavery. They shaped particular, delimited race/gender identities of slaves and European settlers. In the United States, a gradual shift occurred from usage of the common term for settlers, "Christian," to those of "English" and "free." After about 1680, the term "white" emerged for subjective identity in the colonies.[19]

The interweaving of slavery and race/gender made new narratives and political and subjective practices possible. They comprised part of the context of abstract individualism. New narratives in which the American is "new, white, and male" were developed.[20] Once modern ideas of race/gender emerged, enslaved persons were seen as radically other than their masters. "Individual" means, in part, not-slave. The characteristics of the new American—"autonomy, authority, newness and difference, absolute power"—each are "made possible by, shaped by, activated by a complex awareness and employment of a constituted Africanism."[21] Slavery provided the defining other for the abstract individual.

Analyzing race/gender also requires rethinking power. Despite the elimination through law of many legal bases of domination, race/gender subordination persists.[22] Race/gender domination is upheld by juridical power, but it is not amenable to legal solutions. The failures of law, especially Supreme Court decisions, to resolve matters of race/gender evidence the inability to legislate an end to relationships of dominance/subordinance. Traditional concepts of power block our grasp of its other causes. Michel Foucault's ideas about biopower and its effects on the formation of subjectivity are essential to understanding this situation.[23]

Race/gender is a prime locus of biopower. The continuing operation of norms and regulations reproduced it. Biopower is a way of organizing bodies. Power transforms certain physical features into formative social facts and ideas. Skin color does not cause our ideas about race any more than genitals give rise to an idea of gender. Once these categories are developed and regulate the lives of subjects, however, expert knowledge works to justify them. Because all subjects live within existing knowledge/power networks, the categories are socially real, and the subjects' bodies have been transformed into social fact. Such an exercise of power is a fundamental problem, and domination based on race/gender cannot be solved by ignoring the social power of its categories. Attempts to attain equality or to offer justice to subordinate groups will not end the domination that reproduces race/gender as a basis of "identity." The entire construction must be dismantled, not to create a race-blind society but to render these categories nonfunctional.

Deconstruction of race/gender categories cannot occur without admitting that a set of relations exists. We cannot pretend that race/gender does not shape us or that we are simply individuals. Even unacknowledged, the categories and practices continue to have formative effects. All of the effects of race/gender on American subjects and institutions must be confronted and undone. This requirement necessitates affirmative action and is a reason that it generates so much anger and resistance. Affirmative action makes every subject's race/gender relevant and incorporates race/gender into dominant institutions. Affirmative action policies force us to face the fact that the contracting subjects of America are not, never were, and cannot be abstract individuals. Until race/gender no longer constructs political subjects, however, no one can devise or implement color-blind policies.

Biopower challenges abstract individualism. Refusing to inquire into how subjects are constituted helps to sustain the myth of the abstract individual. Biopower's subversive effects explain in part the reluctance of dominant groups to integrate it within accounts of contemporary American politics. Attention to biopower exposes the norms and relations of power that produce the "free" subject. Modern beliefs about rationality, freedom, and agency conflict with the effects of the disciplines required to maintain them. The effects of biopower radically transform how we understand the subject of the dominant, legalistic story. The contracting citizen/subject is no longer an abstract, self-constituting, and free agent. Instead this subject is a participating and resisting position within complex circuits of power. Biopower reveals the social production of rationality. It exposes the discipline required to shape beings who can think according to disciplinary norms. These norms emerge out of and regulate many different practices, including psychology, education, and medicine. Such practices shape the "normal" subjects who honor them. Other norms shape the production of knowledge and determine who counts as an expert and thus rightfully exercises power. Rationality without belief in the objectivity of disciplinary, norms jeopardizes social order. If order depends on particular kinds of knowledge and power, its legitimacy is fragile.

From the perspective of biopower, concepts such as Rawls's veil of ignorance acquire an ironic meaning. They imply an unconsciously willful blindness to the social construction of basic principles and the subjects who "discover" them. Law is often deployed as a defense against recognizing these effects of power. In American politics, the meanings of law and justice (both judge and process) are particularly charged. The objectivity of law is essential to the state's stability. Liberal theorists' assertions that discipline is outside of law and that law is neutral rest on wishes that operate to deny the construction of the willing subject and the content of its will. Excluding inquiry into the subject's constitution supports a belief in legal process; however, upholding this belief does not mitigate the inability of these processes to manage or account for the material and subjects actually shaping politics.

One solution to this problem has long been practiced in Western societies. Modern Western states need race/gender categories to protect their legitimating idea of the sovereign subject. To preserve this subject, discipline and rationality are distributed differently along race/gender lines. For people in certain privileged positions, as determined by social relations, race/gender can operate to mask the effects of biopower. Those who are not marked by race/gender can be undetermined by biopower; they can be abstract individuals. Despite biopower, individualism remains a real possibility. The failure to achieve abstract individualism lies in the defects of those who remain marked.

Contemporary theorists disagree about the liberatory potential of features of modern liberalism. Some argue that simultaneous claiming and critique of liberalism are necessary. The abstract individual is necessary to exercise agency. Some collective universal category is essential for emancipatory politics. Only a coherent subject representing sameness can exercise agency or articulate intelligible demands for justice. Without such subjects, race/gender domination cannot be overcome and, because modern Western states claim adherence to rights and individualism, refusing to use these ideas would be self-defeating.

I disagree with these theorists. Their approach propagates race/gender domination. Abstract individualism is a narrative constructed to validate power. This narrative is plausible because it is a story that the powerful want to believe. Denying the effects of narrative and power is dangerous because it enables us to mask the violence required to produce the endings we want.

An exclusive focus on shared oppression obscures the equally important relationships of domination even among subordinates. Not all white women, for example, are situated identically. Why do we so strongly desire to emphasize the commonalities of experience? What motivates the claim that a large part of our shared identity arises from domination? Why are such claims desirable or necessary? Such moves enable white women and black men to ignore their complicity in and privileges of race/gender, heterosexuality, and geographic location. This approach obscures what Wendy Brown calls our "wounded attachments" and the passions that often motivate them—guilt, hate, envy, fear, and resentment.[24] Subjects can simultaneously occupy positions of domination and subordination. One does not have to be a pure victim to resist domination. Only within the logic of abstract individualism does attention to differences among subordinates undermine or weaken claims to race/gender justice. Particularizing subordinates would allow more consideration of the diversity of practices required for justice.

Subject-centered politics—whether of abstract or particular identities—is deeply flawed. The possibility of just practices depends on fuller recognition of the multiple facets of subjectivity and their often tangled, contradictory, and bloody genealogies. Justice and equality cannot remain contingent on identity—on finding some experience or quality (good or bad) that is common to us all. This prohibition applies equally to subordinate and dominant subjects. There is no single, unitary quality that can ground claims to justice. A subject's virtue cannot be the basis for equal treatment. Subject-centered approaches rest on a modern nostalgia for a singular subject of history. We still hope for a purposive history in which time reveals the subject's biography. We want a guaranteed happy ending—the subject's fate is to bring freedom to the world.[25] No such subject exists. Subjects are internally complex, composed of contradictory impulses and material. Subjects are prone to violence and hatred, feelings often interwoven with seemingly opposite ones like love. Dominant and subordinate subjects are equally unstable, overdetermined, and attracted to fantasies of purity and power.

Subject-centered political actions seem almost inevitably to fall into self-defeating traps. They launch us into investigations of a subject's worth and character, and they lead us on a search for the commonalities. These subjects have to be uniform and pure. They become the bearers of the redemptive possibilities for humankind, so they cannot simultaneously be generators of and invested in relationships of domination. Eventually, our contradictory situations as dominators and subordinates clash and provoke two common responses—nihilism and totalitarianism. Both responses permit the dream of purity. The nihilist develops a protective cynicism and detachment. In contrast to purity all is corrupt, believes the nihilist, and thus we are responsible for nothing. The totalitarian refuses to accept the impossibility of purity and assigns the sources of imperfection to others. For the greater good, says the totalitarian, vast force is justified to eradicate the polluting ones.

Instead of depending on a privileged or a redemptive subject as the agent of change, we can develop politics based on a mutual desire for particular objects or outcomes—for example, reduction of domination. A powerful motivation for political activity is attachment by highly diverse subjects to a particular object.[26] This attachment to a particular object makes coalitions both possible and necessary. Diversity does not preclude mutual attachment to particular objects.[27] We may not even share the same reasons for our attachment to a common object. These attachments will unfold and gather force in unpredictable ways. Chance, desire, and circumstance are important forces in politics.

Developing object-centered political strategies offers new possibilities. Complex attachments to particular objects replace subject-centered theories and practices. How do we create such attachments? We must foster a dislike of uniformity and an appreciation of multiplicity. This dislike can be a basis for resisting domination. Multiplicity exists internally within each subject and shapes relationships. Recognition of multiplicity enables us to develop an engaged detachment, which when exercised permits the complex networks of contradictory desires and powers within and between subjects to emerge. Because reason can be used to obscure passions motivating seemingly rational choices, rational thought is not a sufficient or unproblematic way to develop engaged detachment. Instead, engaged detachment requires consistent willingness to confront the multiple differences that shape subjects. Paradoxically, the more we acknowledge our complex desires, the less we are determined by any one of them. Immersion, not abstraction, allows us to be more objective. When we juxtapose our desires, we realize our own internal instabilities and we understand that we must seek out others who appear unlike us. The more possibilities we confront, the more we disrupt the illusion of identity. Part of what each subject realizes in confrontations with others is how we are all differently affected by determining social relationships. We discover that most subjects occupy several places at once—we resist, impose, and suffer as a result of different kinds of power. Engaged detachment leads to clearer thinking about justice. Our desires and social construction are intrinsic, so we cannot escape them. Only intense recognition, as opposed to a veil of ignorance, can provide any distance from their effects. Furthermore, acknowledgment of our enmeshment is required for, not an impediment to, acting justly. We cannot articulate any useful principles or practices of justice outside of particular social contexts. Such practices are designed for and by the persons residing within them.

Justice depends on continual confrontations among subjects. Discourse begins when we acknowledge our status as subjects who simultaneously occupy complex and contradictory positions. In this arrangement, the other is not outside of or foreign to the self. One's subjectivity is simultaneously constituted by otherness—for example, there can be no heterosexual without a corresponding and intrinsically constituting homosexual. Instead of a search for consensus, such interaction intentionally seeks disjunctions. Agreement will not necessary result from such interaction, nor is it the governing purpose. When genuine understanding is reached, unresolvable conflict will result as frequently as empathy, reflective equilibrium, or an ideal speech community.

Until we honestly acknowledge our differences, hatreds, divisions, and the multiplicity of positions as oppressor and oppressed, shared identity can only be interpreted as a wish to control others. Shared identity represents denial of both past and current conflicts in the contemporary United States. Paradoxically, solidarity depends not on identity but on multiplicity. Even only implicit guilty knowledge of the bloody genealogy of our differences contributes to difficulty in imagining how diversity could provide opportunities for constructive social interactions. Denying the conflicts in U. S. history is foolish. The claim that attending to multiplicity is politically dangerous can appeal only to those whose power would be undermined if they abandoned an unmarked, unsituated position. Given the history of social relations in the United States, such a principle could operate only to recertify the asymmetries that exist.

Until there are fundamental redistributions of power among races, genders, and sexes, the cry made by some writers of "too much difference" must be considered suspect. Justice is undermined by domination, not by multiplicity.[28] To develop a shared future, we must cultivate new, unplatonic loves of diversity, of conflict, and of unshared experiences. Cultivating these loves will require what Bonnie Honig calls an "agonistic" politics,[29] a politics for which conflict and struggle are the norm. We will have to develop a more realistic and interconnected sense of history, subjectivity, and human powers than has prevailed in U. S. political history.

Denial of multiplicity renders claims of solidarity suspect, especially among those who rightfully cannot trust people who see themselves as outside of injustice. White subjects should take responsibility for deconstructing identity/difference: They must render their identities, experiences, and moral categories problematic to themselves, and others. They need to explore the ways in which their subjectivities require negating or denigrating subordinates. Until white subjects participate in such deconstruction, subordinates will have reason to expect action in bad faith. Mutual suspicion and hatred, therefore, will persist.

Because we are all shaped by race/gender, every American is an impure hybrid. We each require an ethic of multiplicity to negotiate our own existences. Multiplicity represents a refusal of identity and difference, two polar entities with meanings determined by a singular logic.[30] Even such multiple subjects cannot serve as ground or guarantee of emancipatory action; they are not simply replacements for unitary subjects. Multiple subjects may act on hatred as readily as on empathy. Hopes for justice rest in what they desire, not on the nature of their identities. Contrary to Rousseau, the freedom we might enjoy depends not on willing the general but on taking responsibility for very particular, context-specific decisions.[31] We must accept that each choice reflects the will of fragile subjects in concert with others in equally tenuous, imperfect, and uncertain situations.

The American polity now confronts a situation with which it is ill-suited to cope. Problems extend beyond denying the differences within U. S. institutions. Even if such denial were terminated, U. S. subjects lack the discursive and political arenas for the free play of multiples. It is more painful to listen to the voices of those marked different and to consider changing social practices than to charge the "others" with undermining "our" order/culture.

Many Americans have only begun to learn to listen to multiple points of view. We are often deaf to the voices of others and blind to the constituting effects of difference in our own subjectivities and politics. Learning to listen is a complex process that requires rethinking one's own position by imagining others' perceptions. This mode of listening is quite different from adopting a Rawlsian veil of ignorance. Behind a veil of ignorance, one impartially tries one point of view after the other and imagines a variety of circumstances, relationships, or rules. None of these adopted perspectives constitutes the self, and the self is not implicated in their existence. They come from the outside, are subjected to rational scrutiny, and are adopted or rejected depending on whether they can be universalized. In this process, the subject mediates between reason and external experience.

The mode of listening I recommend requires an uncomfortable, double consciousness.[32] The marked bearers of cultural differences have extensive experience with this type of listening. One must see oneself as others do. The others' views cannot be totally alien or external because they have constituting effects. One must struggle with and against them until the struggle becomes part of one's subjectivity. Like the effects of the unconscious, one can never be fully aware of the effects of the others' views or of the relationships of power that energize their views. Even aspects of subjectivity that seem fully self-determining are suspect—one can never fully trust oneself. Decentered, estranged, multiple, overdetermined subjectivity is not a postmodernist conceit. Colonized others—culturally, racially, or sexually defined—have long been familiar with this type of subjectivity, whereas persons of relative privilege are not required to adopt this double consciousness.[33] For the privileged, exercising double consciousness requires empathy and a willingness to see oneself as a contextual, situationally determined subject. It requires recognition of the dependence of one's own identity on the other.

Abstract individualism and identity politics are merely two variants of the same logic. Both are forms of identity politics; only their ideal subjects differ. The subject of the first is purely abstract and of the second, purely concrete. The only promising alternative to the failures of identity politics is rejecting the ideas and practices that demand unitary concepts of subjectivity, identity, and difference. We must think about difference in new ways. It is neither a container for all that identity is not nor an alternate basis of unity. Going beyond these associations provides spaces for multiplicity. Gilroy provides several creative avenues for constructing such spaces. He emphasizes the need to theorize about culture outside of absolute, immutable ethnic differences. He writes, "Modernity might be thought to begin in the constitutive relationships with outsiders that both found and temper a self-conscious sense of western civilization.[34] Gilroy suggests that we rethink modernity via the history of the "Black Atlantic," a "'webbed network, between the local and the global."[35] The web is woven via ships and the slave trade among Africa, the Caribbean, Europe, and the Americas. The African diaspora into the Western hemisphere is thus a constituting force within European American histories and identities.

Gilroy's view "challenges the coherence of all narrow nationalist perspectives and points to the spurious invocation of ethnic particularity to enforce them and to ensure the tidy flow of cultural output into neat, symmetrical units. . . . This applies whether this impulse comes from the oppressor or the oppressed."[36] The diaspora has constituting effects on the subjectivities of everyone within the web. Rejecting Africa/Europe and white/black binaries for roots and rootedness, Gilroy substitutes incessant travel, the middle passage, and unstable identities produced by processes of movement and mediation. Diasporian histories address the effect on modernity and subjectivities of exile, relocation, and displacement. Intrinsic to these histories is a desire to escape the structures of the state and the constraints of ethnicity and national particularity. Postmodern subjects inhabit the black Atlantic uneasily, but its web weaves us all into increasingly complex patterns of impure, restless, and rootless subjectivities.

Rethinking of history is precisely what did not occur in the Thomas hearings. The hearings replicated some of the great consequences of difference in liberal politics: experience creates differences, which create special histories and sensitivities. Consequently, justice requires attention to these histories and amelioration of some of their consequences; however, justice also requires objectivity and equal treatment. In this scenario, one cannot be objective *and* empirically determined. To be included, the different must be the same. How can the different simply be added to the same? It cannot; it must be deraced. The different remains marked as other and potentially disruptive. A history of domination again becomes the black man's burden. *Black* men cannot be Supreme Court justices, but the appointment of a black man to the Supreme Court affirms that the system is and must remain race blind.

While grappling with race/gender, the senators illustrated the fundamental dilemmas of American politics. Instabilities result from avoiding race/gender asymmetries, but addressing the instabilities also endangers existing institutions. One possible solution is to expel or neutralize the undermining of others who are not willing to neutralize oneself. The marking of the committee's race/gender position was momentary. It quickly receded into the background. The usual inhabitant, a black/male, occupied the marked race/gender position. Admission to power within American political institutions required the unmarking (whiting out) of its agents. Abstract individualism quickly accomplished this unmarking. Through speech acts, Thomas was transmuted by his values into an honorary and honorable individual who refused his marking. Like all rugged individuals, he set his own goals.

Most of the senators engaged in this type of speaking. Senator Warner's written statement for the committee articulated the dominant themes, processes, and characteristics of the first hearing. Warner commended Thomas's values and character.

> [Thomas' values] are a direct reflection of his background—a background of which he speaks to me with pride. Clarence Thomas was raised in a poor, segregated environment in a small town in Georgia. His grandfather, a strong, self-educated man who was determined that his grandson would have more opportunities than he himself had experienced, firmly instilled in Clarence the virtues of hard work, diligence, tenacity, and religious values. Most importantly, he impressed upon him that he should not use the circumstances of his upbringing as an excuse of not striving to achieve excellence in his own goals. Judge Thomas further expresses with humility and gratitude the support given by religious teachers throughout his life time. Judge Thomas has truly experienced poverty, prejudice, and racism in his life time, but true to those who have inspired him, he has set his own goals. (Committee 1:87–88)

Danforth made a similar point. He described Thomas's attitude throughout the period in which he was in Danforth's employ:

Clarence made it clear he was his own person, to be judged on his own merits. He was not to be the special case, given special treatment, and he was not to be given special work with my office. He was uniquely Clarence Thomas, and his goal was to be the best Clarence Thomas he could possibly be. He has reached that goal and that to me is his most striking attribute. (Committee 1:96)

Thomas and the senators shared the values of rugged masculinity and a willingness to disguise their race/gender specificity behind the mask of the abstract individual. They formed an alliance based on the need for male mentors and models. Black/males without stalwart grandfathers such as Thomas's or mentors like Danforth are likely to end up in prison, they suggested. Ultimately each subject creates and is responsible for his own fate, and opportunity is available to those enterprising enough to seize it, they implied. Even before Anita Hill's charges were publicized, their bond foreclosed any narrative space for her story. As the hearings concluded, abstract individualism temporarily succeeded in warding off the threats of internal chaos, but this success came at a terrible cost. Disregarding multiplicity never eliminates it. The hearings should remind us that subjective construction is a political art and that our narratives matter. American subjects cannot erase the looming costs of their dream.

BIBLIOGRAPHY

Aeschylus. "The Eumenides." In *The Oresteian Trilogy*. New York: Penguin, 1956.

Alger, Horatio. *Mark, the Match Boy*. New York: Collier, 1962.

Alger, Horatio. *Ragged Dick*. New York: Collier, 1962.

Anzaldua, Gloria, ed. *Making Face, Making Soul—Haciendo Caras: Creative and Critical Perspectives by Women of Color*. San Francisco: Aunt Lute, 1990.

Appiah, Kwame Anthony. *in My Father's House: Africa in the Philosophy of Culture*. New York: Oxford University Press, 1992.

Avineri, Shlomo, and Avner de-Shalit, eds. *Communitarianism and Individualism*. New York: Oxford University Press 1992.

Baldwin, James. *The Price of the Ticket*. New York: St. Martin's, 1985.

Barker, Lucius J. "Limits of Political Strategy: A Systemic View of the African American Experience." *American Political Science Review* 88, 1 (1994): 1–14.

Barker, Lucius J., and Jesse J. McCorry, Jr. *Black Americans and the Political System*. Cambridge: Winthrop Publishers, 1980.

Bell, Derrick. *And We Are Not Saved: The Elusive Quest for Racial Justice*. New York: Basic Books, 1987.

Bell, Derrick. *Faces at the Bottom of the Well: The Permanence of Racism*. New York: Basic Books, 1992.

Bellah, Robert N., et al. *Habits of the Heart*. New York: Harper & Row, 1986.

Benhabib, Seyla, and Drucilla Cornell, eds. *Feminism as Critique*. Minneapolis: University of Minnesota Press, 1987.

Blauner, Bob. *Black Lives, White Lives: Three Decades of Race Relations in America*. Berkeley: University of California Press, 1990.

Blount, Marcellus, and George P. Cunningham. *Representing Black Men*. New York: Routledge, 1996.

Braidotti, Rosi. *Patterns of Dissonance*. New York: Routledge, 1991.

Brown, Wendy. *Manhood and Politics: A Feminist Reading in Political Theory*, Totowa, N.J.: Rowman & Littlefield, 1988.

Brown, Wendy. *States of Injury: Power and Freedom in Late Modernity.* Princeton: Princeton University Press, 1995.

Brown, Wendy. "Wounded Attachments." *Political Theory* 21,3 (1993): 390–410.

Burchell, Graham, Colin Gordon, and Peter Miller, eds. *The Foucault Effect: Studies in Governmentality.* Chicago: University of Chicago Press, 1991.

Butler, Judith. *Bodies That Matter: On the Discursive Limits of "Sex."* New York: Routledge, 1993.

Butler, Judith. *Gender Trouble: Feminism and the Subversion of Identity.* New York: Routledge, 1990.

Butler, Judith, and Joan W. Scott, eds. *Feminists Theorize the Political.* New York: Routledge, 1992.

Caraway, Nancy. *Segregated Sisterhood: Racism and the Politics of American Feminism.* Knoxville: University of Tennessee Press, 1991.

Carby, Hazel. *Reconstructing Womanhood: The Emergence of the Afro-American Woman Novelist.* New York: Oxford University Press, 1987.

Collins, Patricia Hill. *Black Feminist Thought: Knowledge, Consciousness, and the Politics of Empowerment.* New York: Routledge, 1991.

Committee on the Judiciary, United States Senate. *Nomination of Judge Clarence Thomas to Be Associate Justice of the Supreme Court.* Washington: Government Printing Office, 1993.

Connolly, William E. *Political Theory and Modernity.* New York: Blackwell, 1988.

Cornell, Drucilla, Michel Rosenfeld, and David Gray Carlson, eds. *Deconstruction and the Possibility of Justice.* New York: Routledge, 1992.

Cose, Ellis. *The Rage of a Priviledged Class.* New York: Harper Collins, 1993.

Crenshaw, Kimberle. "Whose Story Is It, Anyway? Feminist and Antiracist Appropriations of Anita Hill." In *Race-ing Justice, Engendering Power,* ed. Toni Morrison. New York: Pantheon, 1992.

Davis, Angela Y. *Women, Race & Class.* New York: Random House, 1981.

Davis, James F. *Who Is Black?: One Nation's Definition.* University Park: Pennsylvania State University Press, 1991.

Delgado, Richard, ed. *Critical Race Theory: The Cutting Edge.* Philadelphia: Temple University Press, 1995.

Di Stephano, Christine. *Configurations of Masculinity: A Feminist Perspective on Modern Political Theory.* Ithaca: Cornell University Press, 1991.

DuBois, W. E. Burghardt. *The Souls of Black Folk.* New York: Fawcett, 1961.

duCille, Ann. "The Occult of True Womanhood: Critical Demeanor and Black Feminist Studies." *Signs* 19, 3 (1994): 591–629.

Eisenstein, Zillah R. *The Radical Future of Liberal Feminism.* New York: Longman, 1981.

Ellison, Ralph. *The Collected Essays of Ralph Ellison.* New York: Modern Library, 1995.

Euben, Peter J. *The Tragedy of Political Theory: The Road Not Taken.* Princeton: Princeton University Press, 1990.

Ezekiel, Raphael S. *The Racist Mind: Portraits of American Neo-Nazis and Klansmen.* New York: Viking, 1995.

Fairbairn, W. Ronald D. "Schizoid Factors in the Personality." In *Psychoanalytic Studies of the Personality,* ed. W. Ronald D. Fairbairn. London: Routledge, 1952.

Ferguson, Kathy. *The Man Question in Feminism.* Berkeley: University of California Press, 1955.

Flax, Jane. *Disputed Subjects: Essays on Pyschoanalysis, Politics, and Philosophy.* New York: Routledge, 1993.

Fout, John C., and Maura Shaw Tantillo, eds. *American Sexual Politics: Sex, Gender and Race Since the Civil War.* Chicago: University of Chicago Press, 1993.

Foucault, Michel. *The History of Sexuality.* Volume 1. New York: Vintage, 1980.

Foucault, Michel. *Power/Knowledge.* New York: Pantheon, 1980.

Frankenberg, Ruth. *White Women, Race Matters: The Social Construction of Whiteness.* Minneapolis: University of Minnesota Press, 1993.

Fraser, Nancy. *Unruly Practices: Power, Discourse, and Gender in Contemporary Social Theory.* Minneapolis: University of Minnesota Press, 1989.

Fraser, Nancy, and Linda Gordon. "A Genealogy of Dependency: Tracing a Keyword of the U.S. Welfare State." *Signs* 19, 3(1994): 309–336.

Friedman, Susan Stanford. "Beyond White and Other: Relationality and Narratives of Race in Feminist Discourse." *Signs* 21, 1 (1995): 1–49.

Freud, Sigmund. *Civilization and Its Discontents.* New York: W. W. Norton, 1961.

Freud, Sigmund. *Group Psychology and the Analysis of the Ego.* New York: W. W. Norton, 1959.

Freud, Sigmund. *Totem and Taboo.* New York: W. W. Norton, 1950.

Fuss, Diana. *Essentially Speaking: Feminism, Nature and Difference.* New York: Routledge, 1989.

Gates, Henry Louis, Jr., ed. *"Race," Writing, and Difference.* Chicago: University of Chicago Press, 1986.

Giddings, Paula. *When and Where I Enter: The Impact of Black Women on Race and Sex in America.* New York: Bantam, 1984.

Gilroy, Paul. *The Black Atlantic: Modernity and Double Consciousness.* Cambridge: Harvard University Press, 1993.

Goldberg, David Theo. *Racist Culture: Philosophy and the Politics of Meaning.* Cambridge: Blackwell, 1993.

Goldberg, David Theo. "The Social Formation of Racist Discourse." In *Anatomy of Racism*, ed. David Theo Goldberg. Minneapolis: University of Minnesota Press, 1990.

Golden, Thelma, ed. *Black Male: Representations of Masculinity in Contemporary Art.* New York: Whitney Museum, 1994.

Hacker, Andrew. *Two Nations: Black and White, Separate, Hostile and Unequal.* New York: Charles Scribners, 1992.

Hampshire, Stuart. *Innocence and Experience.* Cambridge: Harvard University Press, 1989.

Hartsock, Nancy C. M. *Money, Sex and Power: Toward a Feminist Materialism.* Boston: Northeastern University Press, 1985.

Hegel, G. W. F. *The Phenomenology of Mind.* New York: Harper, 1967.

Higgenbotham, Evelyn Brooks. "African-American Women's History and the Metalanguage of Race." *Signs* 17, 2(1992): 251–274.

Hill, Anita. *Speaking Truth to Power.* New York: Doubleday, 1997.

Hill, Anita Faye, and Emma Coleman Jordan, eds. *Race, Gender, and Power in America: The Legacy of the Hill–Thomas Hearings.* New York: Oxford University Press, 1995.

Hirschman, Nancy. *Rethinking Obligation: A Feminist Method for Political Theory.* Ithaca: Cornell University Press, 1992.

Hochschild, Jennifer L. *Facing up to the American Dream: Race, Class and the Soul of the Nation.* Princeton: Princeton University Press, 1995.

Honig, Bonnie. *Political Theory and the Displacement of Politics.* Ithaca: Cornell University Press, 1993.

hooks, bell. *Feminist Theory: From Margin to Center.* Boston: South End Press, 1984.

hooks, bell. *Killing Rage: Ending Racism.* New York: Henry Holt, 1995.

hooks, bell. *Yearning: Race, Gender, and Cultural Politics.* Boston: South End Press, 1990.

Irigaray, Luce. "Commodities Among Themselves." In *This Sex Which Is Not One*, ed. Luce Irigaray. Ithaca. Cornell University Press, 1985.

James, Stanlie M., and Abena P. A. Busa, eds. *Theorizing Black Feminisms: The Visionary Pragmatism of Black Women.* New York: Routledge, 1993.

Jones, Kathleen B., and Anna G. Jonasdottir, eds. *The Political Interests of Gender: Developing Theory and Research with a Feminist Face.* Newbury Park, Calif.: Sage, 1988.

Jordan, Winthrop D. *White over Black: American Attitudes to the Negro, 1650–1812.* New York. W. W. Norton, 1977.

King, Deborah K. "Multiple Jeopardy, Multiple Consciousness: The Context of Black Feminist Thought." In *Black Women in America: Social Science Perspectives*, ed. M. Malson et al. Chicago: University of Chicago Press, 1990.

Lam, Maivan Clech. "Feeling Foreign in Feminism." *Signs* 19, 4(1994): 865–893.

Landes, Joan R. *Women and the Public Sphere in the Age of the French Revolution.* Ithaca: Cornell University Press, 1988.

Laqueur, Thomas. *Making Sex: Body and Gender from the Greeks to Freud.* Cambridge: Harvard University Press, 1990.

Leary, Kimberlyn. "Race in Psychoanalytic Space." *Gender & Psychoanalysis* 2, 2(1997): 157–172.

Levi-Strauss, Claude. *The Elementary Structures of Kinship.* Boston: Beacon, 1969.

Locke, John. *Two Treatises of Government.* New York: Cambridge University Press, 1965.

Lott, Eric. *Love & Theft: Blackface Minstrelsy and the American Working Class.* New York: Oxford University Press, 1993.

Lubiano, Wahneema. "Black Ladies, Welfare Queens, and State Minstrels: Ideological War by Narrative Means." In *Race-ing Justice, En-gendering Power,* ed. Toni Morrison. New York: Pantheon, 1992.

Lugones, Maria. "Purity, Impurity, and Separation." *Signs* 19, 3(1994): 458–479.

MacCannell, Juliet Flower. *The Regime of the Brother: After the Patriarchy.* New York: Routledge, 1991.

MacKinnon, Catherine A. *Feminism Unmodified: Discourses on Life and Law.* Cambridge: Harvard University Press, 1987.

Malson, Micheline R., Elisabeth Mudimbe-Boyl, Jean F. O'Barr, and Mary Wyer, eds. *Black Women in America: Social Science Perspectives.* Chicago: University of Chicago Press, 1988.

Mayer, Jane, and Jill Abramson. *Strange Justice: The Selling of Clarence Thomas.* New York: Houghton Mifflin, 1994.

McKay, Nellie. "Acknowledging Differences: Can Women Find Unity Through Diversity?" In *Theorizing Black Feminisms: The Visionary Pragmatism of Black Women,* ed. Stanlie M. James and Abena P. A. Busa. New York: Routledge, 1993.

Martin, Biddy, and Chandra Talpade Mohanty. "Feminist Politics: What's Home Got to Do with It?" In *Feminist Studies/Critical Studies,* ed. Teresa de Lauretis. Bloomington: Indiana University Press, 1986.

Martin, Luther H., Huck Gutman, and Patrick Hutton. *Technologies of the Self: A Seminar with Michel Foucault.* Amherst: University of Massachusetts Press, 1988.

Mills, Charles W. *The Racial Contract.* Ithaca: Cornell University Press, 1997.

Minh-ha, Trinh T. *Woman/Native/Other.* Bloomington: Indiana University Press, 1989.

Molina, Maria Luisa "Pupsa." "Fragmentations: Mediations on Separatism." *Signs* 19, 2 (1994): 449–457.

Morrison, Toni. *Beloved.* New York: Signet, 1991.

Morrison, Toni. *Playing in the Dark: Whiteness and the Literary Imagination.* New York: Vintage, 1992.

Morrison, Toni, ed. *Race-ing Justice, En-gendering Power: Essays on Anita Hill, Clarence Thomas and the Construction of Social Reality.* New York: Pantheon, 1992.

Mouffe, Chantal. "Feminism, Citizenship, and Radical Democratic Politics." In *Feminists Theorize the Political,* eds. Judith Butler and Joan W. Scott. New York: Routledge, 1992.

Mouffe, Chantal. *The Return of the Political.* New York: Verso, 1993.

Mudimbe, V. Y. *The Invention of Africa: Gnosis, Philosophy, and the Order of Knowledge.* Indianapolis: Indiana University Press, 1988.

Myrdal, Gunnar. *An American Dilemma.* 2 vols. New York: McGraw-Hill, 1964.

Nicholson, Linda J. *Gender and History: The Limits of Social Theory in the Age of the Family.* New York: Columbia University Press, 1986.

Nicholson, Linda J. "Interpreting Gender." *Signs* 20, 1 (1994): 79–105.

Nye, Andrea. *Feminist Theory and the Philosophies of Man.* New York: Routledge, 1988.

O'Connor, Noreen, and Joanna Ryan. *Wild Desires and Mistaken Identities: Lesbianism and Psychoanalysis.* London: Virago, 1993.

Okin, Susan Moller. *Justice, Gender and the Family.* New York: Basic Books, 1989.

Okin, Susan Moller. "Gender Inequality and Gender Differences." *Political Theory* 22, 1 (1994): 5–24.

Omi, Michael, and Howard Winant. *Racial Formations in the United States: From the 1960's to the 1980's.* New York: Routledge, 1986.

O'Reilly, Kenneth. *Nixon's Piano: Presidents and Racial Politics from Washington to Clinton.* New York: Free Press, 1995.

Painter, Nell Irwin. "Hill, Thomas, and the Use of Racial Stereotype." In *Race-ing Justice, En-gendering Power.* ed. Toni Morrison. New York: Pantheon, 1992.

Pateman, Carole. *The Disorder of Women.* Stanford: Stanford University Press, 1989.

Pateman, Carole. *The Sexual Contract.* Stanford: Stanford University Press, 1988.

Pateman, Carole, and Elizabeth Gross, eds. *Feminist Challenges: Social and Political Theory.* Boston: Northeastern University Press, 1986.

Patterson, Orlando. *Freedom.* Volume 1: *Freedom in the Making of Western Culture.* New York: Basic Books, 1991.

Phillips, Anne. *Engendering Democracy*. University Park: Pennsylvania State University Press, 1991.

Phillips, Anne, ed. *Feminism and Equality*. New York: New York University Press, 1987.

Rabinow, Paul, ed. *The Foucault Reader*. New York: Pantheon, 1984.

Rawls, John. *A Theory of Justice*. Cambridge: Harvard University Press, 1971.

Reagon, Bernice Johnson. "Coalition Politics: Turning the Century." In *Home Girls: A Black Feminist Anthology*, ed. Barbara Smith. New York: Kitchen Table Press, 1983.

Rich, Adrienne. "Compulsory Heterosexuality and Lesbian Existence." *Signs* 5, 4 (1980): 631–660.

Rich, Adrienne. *Of Woman Born: Motherhood as Experience and Institution*. New York: W. W. Norton, 1976.

Rhode, Deborah. *Justice and Gender*. Cambridge: Harvard University Press, 1989.

Rogin, Michael. *Fathers & Children: Andrew Jackson and the Subjugation of the American Indian*. New York: Vintage, 1976.

Rousseau, Jean-Jacques. *The Basic Political Writings*. Indianapolis: Hackett, 1987.

Rousseau, Jean-Jacques. *On the Social Contract*, ed. Roger D. Masters. New York: St. Martin's, 1978.

Rubin, Gayle. "The Traffic in Women: Notes on the 'Political Economy' of Sex." In *Toward an Anthropology of Women*, ed. Rayna R. Reiter. New York: Monthly Review Press, 1975.

Sandel, Michael. *Liberalism and the Limits of Justice*. Cambridge: Harvard University Press, 1982.

Sapiro, Virginia. *The Political Integration of Women: Roles, Socialization and Politics*. Urbana: University of Illinois Press, 1984.

Sklar, Judith. *American Citizenship*. Cambridge: Harvard University Press, 1991.

Smith, Barbara, ed. *Home Girls: A Black Feminist Anthology*. New York: Kitchen Table Press, 1983.

Smitherman, Geneva, ed. *African American Women Speak out on Anita Hill–Clarence Thomas*. Detroit: Wayne State University Press, 1995.

Spelman, Elizabeth V. *Inessential Woman: Problems of Exclusion in Feminist Thought*. Boston: Beacon, 1988.

Stiehm, Judith, ed. *Women's Views of the Political World of Men*. Dobbs Ferry, N.Y.: Transnational Publishers, 1984.

Takaki, Ronald. *Iron Cages: Race and Culture in 19th-Century America*. New York: Oxford University Press, 1990.

Tronto, Joan C. *Moral Boundaries: A Political Argument for an Ethic of Care.* New York: Routledge, 1993.

Washington, Booker T. *Up from Slavery.* New York: Dell, 1965.

Weber, Max. "Politics as a Vocation." In *From Max Weber,* ed. H. H. Gerth and C. Wright Mills. New York: Oxford University Press, 1946.

West, Cornel. *Race Matters.* Boston: Beacon, 1993.

Williams, Patricia J. *The Alchemy of Race and Rights: Diary of a Law Professor.* Cambridge: Harvard University Press, 1991.

Wilson, Midge, and Kathy Russell. *Divided Sisters: Bridging the Gap Between Black Women and White Women.* New York: Anchor Books, 1996.

Winant, Howard. *Racial Conditions: Politics, Theory, Comparisons.* Minneapolis: University of Minnesota Press, 1994.

Wing, Adrien Katherine, ed. *Critical Race Feminism: A Reader.* New York: New York University Press, 1997.

Wolin, Sheldon S. *Politics and Vision: Continuity and Innovation in Western Political Thought.* Boston: Little, Brown, 1960.

Young, Iris Marion. "Gender as Seriality: Thinking about Women as a Social Collective." *Signs* 19, 1 (1994): 713–738.

Young, Iris Marion. *Justice and the Politics of Difference.* Princeton: Princeton University Press, 1990.

Young, Iris Marion. *Throwing Like a Girl and Other Essays in Feminist Philosophy and Social Theory.* Bloomington: Indiana University Press, 1990.

Zack, Naomi. *Race/Sex: Their Sameness, Difference, Interplay.* New York: Routledge, 1997.

Zerilli, Linda. *Signifying Woman: Culture and Chaos in Rousseau, Burke and Mill.* Ithaca: Cornell University Press, 1994.

NOTES

INTRODUCTION: AMERICAN DILEMMAS AND
THE AMERICAN DREAM

1. W. E. Burghart DuBois, *The Souls of Black Folk* (New York: Fawcett, 1961); Winthrop D. Jordan, *White over Black: American Attitudes to the Negro, 1650–1812* (New York: W. W. Norton, 1977); James Baldwin; *The Price of the Ticket* (New York: St. Martin's, 1985); Judith Sklar, *American Citizenship* (Cambridge: Harvard University Press, 1991); Toni Morrison, *Playing in the Dark: Whiteness and the Literary Imagination* (New York: Vintage, 1992); Ralph Ellison, *The Collected Essays of Ralph Ellison* (New York: Modern Library, 1995); Kenneth O'Reilly, *Nixon's Piano: Presidents and Racial Politics from Washington to Clinton* (New York: Free Press, 1995).

2. Kwame Anthony Appiah, *In My Father's House: Africa in the Philosophy of Culture* (New York: Oxford University Press, 1992); Richard Delgado, ed., *Critical Race Theory: The Cutting Edge* (Philadelphia: Temple University Press, 1995); Adrien Katherine Wing, ed., *Critical Race Feminism: A Reader* (New York: New York University Press, 1997); Naomi Zack, *Race/Sex: Their Sameness, Difference, Interplay* (New York: Routledge, 1997).

3. Bob Blauner, *Black Lives, White Lives: Three Decades of Race Relations in America* (Berkeley: University of California Press, 1990); Andrew Hacker, *Two Nations: Black and White, Separate, Hostile and Unequal* (New York: Charles Scribners, 1992).

4. Derrick Bell, *And We Are Not Saved: The Elusive Quest for Racial Justice* (New York: Basic Books, 1987), pp. 34–35.

5. Orlando Patterson, *Freedom*, vol. 1 of *Freedom in the Making of Western Culture* (New York: Basic Books, 1991).

6. Jennifer L. Hochschild, *Facing up to the American Dream: Race, Class and the Soul of the Nation* (Princeton: Princeton University Press, 1995).

7. Barbara Smith, ed., *Home Girls: A Black Feminist Anthology* (New York:

Kitchen Table Press, 1983); Elizabeth V. Spelman, *Inessential Woman: Problems of Exclusion in Feminist Thought* (Boston: Beacon, 1988); Diana Fuss, *Essentially Speaking: Feminism, Nature and Difference* (New York: Routledge, 1989); bell hooks, *Yearning: race, gender and cultural politics* (Boston: South End Press, 1990); bell hooks, *Killing Rage: Ending Racism* (New York: Henry Holt, 1995); Ruth Frankenberg, *White Women, Race Matters; The Social Construction of Whiteness* (Minneapolis: University of Minnesota Press, 1993); Thelma Golden, ed., *Black Male: Representations of Masculinity in Contemporary Art* (New York: Whitney Museum, 1994); Midge Wilson and Kathy Russell, *Divided Sisters: Bridging the Gap Between Black Women and White Women* (New York: Anchor Books, 1996); Marcellus Blount and George P. Cunningham, *Representing Black Men* (New York: Routledge, 1996).

8. Evelyn Brooks Higgenbotham, "African-American Women's History and the Metalanguage of Race," *Signs* 17, 2 (1992): 251–274; Maria Lugones, "Purity, Impurity and Separation," *Signs* 19, 3 (1994): 458–479.

9. Michael Omi and Howard Winant, *Racial Formations in the United States: From the 1960's to the 1980's* (New York: Routledge, 1996), p. 61.

10. Ronald Takaki, *Iron Cages: Race and Culture in 19th-Century America* (New York: Oxford University Press, 1990).

11. Toni Morrison, ed., *Race-ing Justice, En-gendering Power: Essays on Anita Hill, Clarence Thomas, and the Construction of Social Reality* (New York: Pantheon, 1992); Jane Mayer and Jill Abramson, *Strange Justice: The Selling of Clarence Thomas* (New York: Houghton Mifflin, 1994); Anita Faye Hill and Emma Coleman Jordan, eds., *Race, Gender, and Power in America: The Legacy of the Hill-Thomas Hearings* (New York: Oxford University Press, 1995); Geneva Smitherman, ed., *African American Women Speak out on Anita Hill-Clarence Thomas* (Detroit: Wayne State University Press, 1995); Anita Hill, *Speaking Truth to Power* (New York: Doubleday, 1997).

12. Michael Rogin, *Fathers & Children: Andrew Jackson and the Subjugation of the American Indian* (New York: Vintage, 1976).

13. Kimberlyn Leary, "Race in Psychoanalytic Space," *Gender & Psychoanalysis* 2, 2 (1997): 157–172.

14. Eric Lott, *Love & Theft: Blackface Minstrelsy and the American Working Class* (New York: Oxford University Press, 1993).

15. Deborah Rhode, *Justice and Gender* (Cambridge: Harvard University Press, 1989).

16. Carole Pateman, *The Sexual Contract* (Stanford: Stanford University Press, 1988).

17. Judith Butler, *Gender Trouble: Feminism and the Subversion of Identity* (New York: Routledge, 1990); Judith Butler, *Bodies That Matter: On the*

Discursive Limits of "Sex" (New York: Routledge, 1993); Adrienne Rich, "Compulsory Heterosexuality and Lesbian Existence," *Signs* 5, 4 (1980): 631–660; Michel Foucault, *The History of Sexuality*. Volume 1. (New York: Vintage, 1980); Thomas Laqueur, *Making Sex: Body and Gender from the Greeks to Freud* (Cambridge: Harvard University Press, 1990); John C. Fout and Maura Shaw Tantillo, eds., *American Sexual Politics: Sex, Gender and Race Since the Civil War* (Chicago: University of Chicago Press, 1993); Noreen O'Connor and Joanna Ryan, *Wild Desires and Mistaken Identities: Lesbianism and Psychoanalysis* (London: Virago, 1993).

18. Seyla Benhabib and Drucilla Cornell, eds., *Feminism as Critique* (Minneapolis: University of Minnesota Press, 1987); Rosi Braidotti, *Patterns of Dissonance* (New York: Routledge, 1991); Wendy Brown, *Manhood and Politics: A Feminist Reading in Political Theory* (Totowa, N.J.: Rowman & Littlefield, 1988); Wendy Brown, "Wounded Attachments," *Political Theory* 21 3 (1993): 390–410; Judith Butler and Joan W. Scott, eds., *Feminists Theorize the Political* (New York: Routledge, 1992); Hazel Carby, *Reconstructing Womanhood: The Emergence of the Afro-American Woman Novelist* (New York: Oxford University Press, 1987); Patricia Hill Collins, *Black Feminist Thought: Knowledge, Consciousness and the Politics of Empowerment* (New York: Routledge, 1991); Angela Y. Davis, *Women, Race & Class* (New York: Random House, 1981); Christine Di Stefano, *Configurations of Masculinity: A Feminist Perspective on Modern Political Theory* (Ithaca: Cornell University Press, 1991); Zillah R. Eisenstein, *The Radical Future of Liberal Feminism* (New York: Longman, 1981); Kathy Ferguson, *The Man Question in Feminism* (Berkeley: University of California Press, 1995); Jane Flax, *Disputed Subjects: Essays on Psychoanalysis, Politics, and Philosophy* (New York: Routledge, 1993); Nancy Fraser, *Unruly Practices: Power, Discourse and Gender in Contemporary Social Theory* (Minneapolis: University of Minnesota Press, 1989); Paula Giddings, *When and Where I Enter: The Impact of Black Women on Race and Sex in America* (New York: Bantam, 1984); Nancy C. M. Hartsock, *Money, Sex and Power: Toward a Feminist Materialism* (Boston: Northeastern University Press, 1985); Nancy Hirschman, *Rethinking Obligation: A Feminist Method for Political Theory* (Ithaca: Cornell University Press, 1992); bell hooks, *Feminist Theory: From Margin to Center* (Boston: South End Press, 1984); Luce Irigaray, "Commodities Among Themselves." In *This Sex Which Is Not One*, ed. Luce Irigaray (Ithaca: Cornell University Press, 1985); Stanlie M. James and Abena P. A. Busa, eds., *Theorizing Black Feminisms: The Visionary Pragmatism of Black Women* (New York: Routledge, 1993); Kathleen B. Jones and Anna G. Jonasdottir, eds., *The Political Interests of Gender: Developing Theory and Research with a Feminist Face* (Newbury Park,

Calif.: Sage, 1988); Joan R. Landes, *Women and the Public Sphere in the Age of the French Revolution* (Ithaca: Cornell University Press, 1988); Juliet Flower MacCannell, *The Regime of the Brother: After the Patriarchy* (New York: Routledge, 1991); Catherine A. MacKinnon, *Feminism Unmodified: Discourses on Life and Law* (Cambridge: Harvard University Press, 1987); Micheline R. Malson, Elisabeth Mudimbe-Boyl, Jean F. O'Barr, and Mary Wyer, eds., *Black Women in America: Social Science Perspectives* (Chicago: University of Chicago Press, 1988); Trinh T. Minh-ha, *Woman/Native Other* (Bloomington: Indiana University Press, 1989); Chantal Mouffe, *The Return of the Political* (New York: Verso, 1993); Linda Nicholson, *Gender and History: The Limits of Social Theory in the Age of the Family* (New York: Columbia University Press, 1986); Andrea Nye, *Feminist Theory and the Philosophies of Man* (New York: Routledge, 1988); Susan Moller Okin, *Justice, Gender and the Family* (New York: Basic Books, 1989); Carole Pateman and Elizabeth Gross, eds., *Feminist Challenges: Social and Political Theory* (Boston: Northeastern University Press, 1986); Carole Pateman, *The Disorder of Women* (Stanford: Stanford University Press, 1989); Anne Phillips, ed., *Feminism and Equality* (New York: New York University Press, 1987); Anne Phillips, *Engendering Democracy* (University Park: Pennsylvania State University Press, 1991); Adrienne Rich, *Of Woman Born: Motherhood as Experience and Institution* (New York: W. W. Norton, 1976); Virginia Sapiro, *The Political Integration of Women: Roles, Socialization and Politics* (Urbana: University of Illinois Press, 1984); Judith Stiehm, ed., *Women's Views of the Political World of Men* (Dobbs Ferry, N.Y.: Transnational Publishers, 1984); Joan C. Tronto, *Moral Boundaries: A Political Argument for an Ethic of Care* (New York: Routledge, 1993); Patricia J. Williams, *The Alchemy of Race and Rights: Diary of a Law Professor* (Cambridge: Harvard University Press, 1991); Iris Marion Young, *Justice and the Politics of Difference* (Princeton: Princeton University Press, 1990); Linda Zerilli, *Signifying Woman: Culture and Chaos in Rousseau, Burke and Mill* (Ithaca: Cornell University Press, 1994).

19. Graham Burchell, Colin Gordon, and Peter Miller, eds., *The Foucault Effect: Studies in Governmentality* (Chicago: University of Chicago Press, 1991); Paul Rabinow, ed., *The Foucault Reader* (New York: Pantheon, 1984).

20. Henry Louis Gates, Jr., ed., *"Race," Writing, and Difference* (Chicago: University of Chicago Press, 1986); Fuss, *Essentially Speaking;* Bell, *And We Are Not Saved;* Derrick Bell, *Faces at the Bottom of the Well: The Permanence of Racism* (New York: Basic Books, 1992); Williams, *The Alchemy of Race and Rights;* Cornel West, *Race Matters* (Boston: Beacon, 1993).

21. Charles W. Mills, *The Racial Contract* (Ithaca: Cornell University Press, 1997).
22. Giddings, *When and Where I Enter;* Kimberle Crenshaw, "Whose Story Is It, Anyway?": Feminist and Antiracist Appropriations of Anita Hill," in Toni Morrison, ed., *Race-ing Justice* En-gendering Power (New York: Pantheon, 1992); Williams, *The Alchemy of Race and Rights.*

CHAPTER 1: AMERICAN DREAM OR NIGHTMARE? HORATIO ALGER AND RACE(D) MEN

1. W. E. Burghardt DuBois, *The Souls of Black Folk* (New York: Fawcett, 1961).

CHAPTER 2: THE MALE/AFRICANIST PRESENCE: SENATORIAL REPRESENTATIONS

1. Toni Morrison, *Playing in the Dark: Whiteness and the Literary Imagination.* (New York: Vintage, 1992).
2. Gunnar Myrdal, *An American Dilemma,* 2 Vols. (New York: McGraw Hill, 1964).

CHAPTER 3: THE FEMALE/AFRICANIST PRESENCE: MALE BONDING IN CONTEMPORARY AMERICAN POLITICS

1. Aeschylus, "The Eumenides," in Aeschylus. *The Oresteian Trilogy* (New York: Penguin, 1956).

CHAPTER 6: "AT LEAST MCCARTHY WAS ELECTED": FRATERNAL RECONCILIATION

1. Claude Levi-Strauss, *The Elementary Structures of Kinship* (Boston: Beacon, 1969); Gayle Rubin, "The Traffic in Women: Notes on the 'Political Economy' of Sex; in Rayna R. Reiter ed., *Toward an Anthropology of Women* (New York: Monthly Review Press, 1975).

CHAPTER 8: WHY RACE / GENDER DOMINATION
PERSISTS: THE NECESSARY FAILURES OF ABSTRACT
INDIVIDUALISM AND IDENTITY POLITICS

1. Michael Sandel, *Liberalism and the Limits of Justice* (Cambridge: Harvard University Press, 1982); Robert N. Bellah, et al., *Habits of the Heart* (New York: Harper & Row, 1996); Shlomo Avineri and Avner de-Shalit, eds., *Communitarianism and Individualism* (New York: Oxford University Press, 1992).
2. W. Ronald D. Fairbairn, "Schizoid Factors in the Personality," in W. Ronald D. Fairbairn, ed., *Psychoanalytic Studies of the Personality* (London: Routledge, 1992).
3. David Theo Goldberg, "The Social Formation of Racist Discourse," in David Theo Goldberg, ed., *Anatomy of Racism* (Minneapolis: University of Minnesota Press, 1990), p. 311.
4. James Baldwin, *The Price of the Ticket* (New York: St. Martin's, 1985); Ralph Ellison. *The Collected Essays of Ralph Ellison* (New York: Modern Library, 1995).
5. Toni Morrison, *Playing in the Dark: Whiteness and the Literary Imagination* (New York: Vintage, 1992), p. 47.
6. Charles W. Mills, *The Racial Contract* (Ithaca: Cornell University Press, 1997), p. 19.
7. John Rawls, *A Theory of Justice* (Cambridge: Harvard University Press, 1971).
8. Maivan Clech Lam, "Feeling Foreign in Feminism," *Signs* 19, 4 (1994): 865–893.
9. David Theo Goldberg, *Racist Culture: Philosophy and the Politics of Meaning* (Cambridge: Blackwell, 1993).
10. James F. Davis, *Who Is Black?: One Nation's Definition* (University Park: Pennsylvania State University, 1991).
11. Ellis Cose, *The Rage of a Privileged Class* (New York: Harper Collins, 1993); Goldberg, *Racist Culture;* Howard Winant, *Racial Conditions: Politics, Theories, Comparisons* (Minneapolis: University of Minnesota Press, 1994).
12. Morrison, *Playing in the Dark,* p. 51.
13. Ibid, p. 52.
14. Nell Irwin Painter, "Hill, Thomas, and the Use of Racial Stereotype," in Toni Morrison, ed., *Race-ing Justice, En-gendering Power* (New York: Pantheon, 1992); Eric Lott, *Love & Theft: Blackface Minstrelsy and the American Working Class* (New York: Oxford University Press, 1993).
15. Paul Gilroy, *The Black Atlantic: Modernity and Double Consciousness* (Cambridge: Harvard University Press, 1993), p. 45.

16. Ibid, p. 55.

17. Ibid, p. 49.

18. Morrison, *Playing in the Dark,* p. 38.

19. Winthrop D. Jordan, *White over Black: American Attitudes to the Negro, 1650–1812* (New York: W. W. Norton, 1977).

20. Morrison, *Playing in the Dark,* p. 43.

21. Ibid, p. 44.

22. Lucius J. Barker and Jesse J. McCorry, Jr., *Black Americans and the Political System* (Cambridge: Winthrop Publishers, 1980); Lucius J. Barker, "Limits of Political Strategy: A Systemic View of the African American Experience," *American Political Science Review* 88, 1 (1994): 1–14.

23. Michel Foucault, *Power/Knowledge* (New York: Pantheon, 1980); Paul Rabinow, ed. *The Foucault Reader* (New York: Pantheon, 1984); Luther H. Martin, Huck Gutman, and Patrick Hutton. *Technologies of the Self: A Seminar with Michel Foucault* (Amherst: University of Massachusetts Press, 1988); Graham Burchell, Colin Gordon, and Peter Miller, eds., *The Foucault Effect: Studies in Governmentality* (Chicago: University of Chicago Press, 1991).

24. Wendy Brown, "Wounded Attachments," *Political Theory* 21, 3 (1993): 390–410.

25. William E. Connolly, *Political Theory and Modernity* (New York: Blackwell, 1988).

26. Linda J. Nicholson, "Interpreting Gender," *Signs* 20, 1 (1994): 79–105.

27. Bernice Johnson Reagon, "Coalition Politics: Turning the Century," in Barbara Smith, ed., *Home Girls: A Black Feminist Anthology* (New York: Kitchen Table Press, 1983); Biddy Martin and Chandra Talpade Mohanty, "Feminist Politics: What's Home Got to Do with It?" in Teresa de Lauretis, ed., *Feminist Studies/Critical Studies* (Bloomington: Indiana University Press, 1986); Chantal Mouffe, "Feminism, Citizenship, and Radical Democratic Politics," in Judith Butler and Joan W. Scott, eds., *Feminists Theorize the Political* (New York: Routledge, 1992); Iris Marion Young, "Gender as Seriality: Thinking about Women as a Social Collective," *Signs* 19, 1 (1994): 713–738.

28. Iris Marion Young, *Justice and the Politics of Difference* (Princeton: Princeton University Press, 1990); Iris Marion Young, *Throwing Like a Girl and Other Essays in Feminist Philosophy and Social Theory* (Bloomington: Indiana University Press, 1990); Drucilla Cornell, Michel Rosenfeld, and David Grey Carison, eds. *Deconstruction and the Possibility of Justice* (New York: Routledge, 1992).

29. Bonnie Honig, *Political Theory and the Displacement of Politics* (Ithaca: Cornell University Press, 1993).

30. Susan Stanford Friedman, "Beyond White and Other: Relationality and Narratives of Race in Feminist Discourse," *Signs* 21, 1 (1995): 1–49.

31. Rousseau, Jean-Jacques, *On The Social Contract,* ed. Roger Masters (New York: St. Martin's, 1978).

32. W. E. Burghardt DuBois, *The Souls of Black Folk* (New York: Fawcett, 1961).

33. Gloria Anzaldua, ed., *Making Face, Making Soul—Haciendo Caras: Creative and Critical Perspectives by Women of Color* (San Francisco: Aunt Lute, 1990); Lam, "Feeling Foreign"; Maria Lugones, "Purity, Impurity, and Separation," *Signs* 19, 3 (1994): 458–479; Maria Luisa "Pupsa" Molina, "Fragmentations: Meditations on Separatism," *Signs* 19, 2 (1994): 449–457.

34. Gilroy, *The Black Atlantic,* p. 17.

35. Ibid, p. 29.

36. Ibid.

37. Wahneema Lubiano, "Black Ladies, Welfare Queens, and State Minstrels: Ideological War by Narrative Means," in Toni Morrison, ed. *Racing Justice, En-gendering Power* (New York: Pantheon, 1992).

INDEX

Shakespeare, Simpson's analogy, 67
Shared oppression, 139–140
Simon, Paul, on Thomas's
    inconsistencies, 43
Simpson, Alan
    accusations against Hill, 65
    on Hill's inconsistencies, 78
    on Hill's motives, 53
    on judicial system, 92
    Othello analogy, 94
    on pornographic talk, 80
    on pornography, 79
    on sexual harassment, 72
    Shakespeare analogy, 67
    on slavery, 35–36
    on Thomas as disadvantaged, 34
    on Thomas's innocence, 92
Slavery
    and abstract individualism, 136
    current presence, 4
    and history, 135
    and race/gender, 136
    and U.S. Constitution, 2–3, 12, 36
Spector, Arlen
    on Hill as expert, 61
    on Hill fantasizing, 124
    on pornographic talk, 80
    on racism, 135–36
    role in second hearing, 81
    suspicion of Hill, 77
Splitting, as psychological defense,
    21–22
Stereotype
    black/female, 57
    black/male, 27, 84–86, 104–105
    of Hill, 66–68
    male/female roles, 56–57
    white/female, 57–58
    white/male, 32
Subject-centered politics, 140–141
Subordinate group
    and identity politics, 131–132
    and race/gender position, 36–37,
        39, 84
    and victimization, 131–132
Supreme Court, confirmation hearings.
    See Hearings
Symbolic castration, 87

T
Thomas, Clarence
    and affirmative action, 35–36
    analogy to Horatio Alger, 127
    and black/male stereotype, 84–86
    character defense, 85–86, 105–106
    childhood, 14, 22–23
    and civil rights movement, 23, 26
    compared to Doggett, 115
    compared to Hill, 89
    education, 23
    as fair and neutral, 27, 29–30, 38
    as family man, 95, 108–110, 112–113
    on Fourteenth Amendment, 47
    Hill's allegations against, 54–56
    on hiring women, 106
    inconsistencies, 26, 28, 43–44,
        46–47, 95
    influence of grandfather, 18–20, 22–23,
        107
    lynching metaphor use, 13, 86–87, 88,
        127
    as martyr, 97
    opinion of Hill, 101–102
    as Othello, 94
    on policy positions, 28–29
    on pornographic talk, 87
    race card use, 25–26
    race/gender position, 16, 24–25, 26–27
    as Rawlsian rational liberator, 29
    relationship with Hill, 110–111
    on Roe v. Wade, 47
    second wife, 94
    self-presentation, 20–21, 24, 27–30, 43,
        48, 95
    as sexual harassment expert, 103–104
    as triumph over adversity, 34–35
    as victim, 81, 88, 90, 94–97
Thurmond, Strom, on Thomas, 27

U
United States
    constitution (See Constitution, U.S.)
    founding of, 6–7

V
Values, family, 108–113
Victimization, and subordinates,
    131–132